A first day cover issued for the centenary of Commodore Perry's visit to the islands. Ryukyu Islands, 1953

A Swedish stamp booklet with designs of the warship **Wasa** which sank on her maiden voyage in 1628 and was salvaged 300 years later

A first day cover for the tenth anniversary of the Deutsche Mark. West Germany

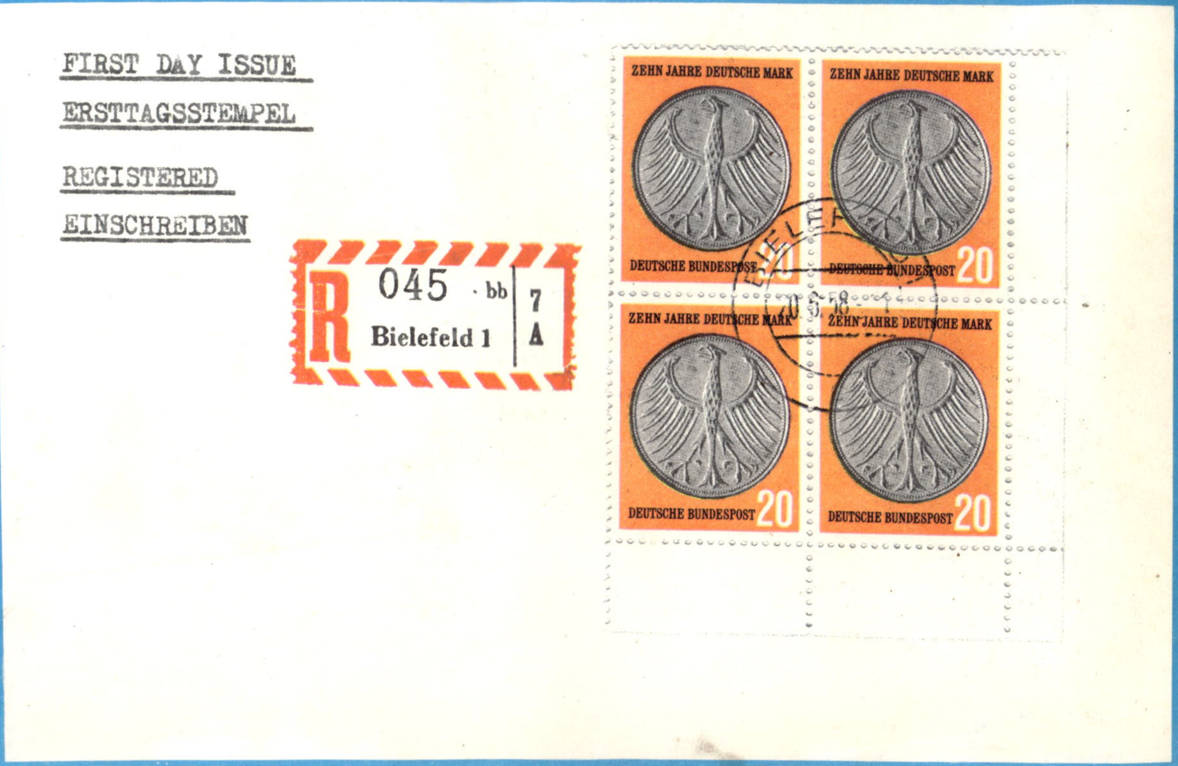

Monsieur Louis Rimand
Paris 17e
AIR MAIL
PAR AVION
A.G.Anderson Esq..
AG Productions

Contents

STAMP COLLECTING all in colour

Text written by:
COLIN NARBETH
JAMES WATSON
BEATRICE COX
KENNETH R. LAKE

First published 1971
Second impression 1971
Third impression 1972
Published by William Collins Sons and Co. Ltd., Glasgow and London

ISBN 0 00 103302 6

Printed by Litografía A. Romero, S. A. Tenerife (Spain)

COLLINS · LONDON AND GLASGOW

Posts of the past

A royal messenger

An early mail cart

Mail steamer

Pony Express rider

Mobile post bus

Mail plane over Washington

The world's oldest adhesive stamps are only a little over 130 years old, but the history of the posts goes back more than three thousand years.

Early messenger systems are mentioned in the Bible, and in ancient Egyptian records telling of runners who delivered messages written on clay or wax tablets.

Credit for the first highly organised system is generally given to King Cyrus the Great of Persia who set up relay posts a day's ride apart, right across his empire from the Mediterranean Sea in the west to India in the east. Mounted couriers sped from relay to relay with his dispatches, logging the time of their arrival at each post.

The Roman emperors had an even more efficient relay system to link them with the furthest corners of their empire. Their couriers were given the fastest horses and chariots to speed them along the new Roman roads. A feather in the cap of the courier identified him as the postal runner and symbolised the speed with which he carried out his duties. Like Cyrus's couriers he carried only official dispatches. The citizens of Rome were forbidden by law to write letters without the Emperor's permission, in case they plotted against him with conspirators outside Rome.

The great princes, merchants and scholars of the Middle Ages each had their own simple messenger system. The ordinary citizens had no regular means of sending messages, but as few could read or write this was not a matter of great concern to them.

As time went by better roads were built, trade increased, and more people learned to read and write. Stage coach services run by private carrier companies took passengers from staging post to staging post, and letters and packages were carried for anyone who could afford the fee.

Slowly these private carrier services developed into national posts run by the various states. And because speed is essential in any postal system, the story of the posts from this point on is very closely linked with the story of transport. The steam train, the motor-car, the steam ship and, later, the aeroplane all brought faster mail services. Today it is possible to send a letter from one side of the world to the other in a matter of days for a very small charge.

Postage stamps were devised as a simple means of paying the posting fee in advance and very soon they were pursued by collectors ready to pay more than face values.

The rare ones

There are several stamps of which only one specimen is known, but by far the most valuable of them all is the 1856 1-cent British Guiana. Unless you happened to know what it was you would not find it very impressive. It is roughly printed, has a creased and careworn look, and its corners are clipped.

It was discovered on an old letter in 1873 by Vernon Vaughan, a local schoolboy. Because there was no place printed for it in his album, he sold it to another collector for six shillings. The stamp has changed hands several times since then. At its last sale, in 1970, it brought $280,000 (almost £120,000) when it was sold to an anonymous buyer.

Europe's most famous rarity is the unique Swedish 1855 3-skilling banco, printed in yellow instead of the usual green. This, too, was found by a schoolboy. He knew that he had found an unusual stamp and got seven kroner for it from a dealer. When last it changed hands the buyer paid close on £30,000.

Wealthy Austrian collector Count von Ferrary was always keen to swap stamps. In 1886 he gave Thomas Tapling a twopenny Mauritius stamp in exchange for a unique pair of Poonch stamps. Today the Mauritius stamp is worth more than £20,000 while the Poonch pair brought £340 when last sold.

When Mauritius printed its first stamps in 1847 – only 500 1d reds and 500 2d blues – it was discovered that the words 'Post Office' had been inscribed on them instead of 'Post Paid', but not before the Governor's wife had already used some of them on invitations to a ball. Today only 14 1d reds and 12 2d blues are known to exist.

The world's first adhesive stamp, Britain's Penny Black of 1840, is not rare. It was issued in millions and many copies still exist. Brazil's 'bull's eyes' of 1843, the world's second national adhesives, are much rarer and much more valuable.

A printer's error produced the most famous American rarity. In 1918 the first U.S. airmails were issued. But one sheet of 24 of the 24-cent stamps sold at a Washington post office showed the aircraft, a Curtiss Jenny, flying upside down. The authorities tried hard to recover the sheet but failed, and the buyer sold it for $15,000. Today each stamp is worth $20,000.

Other valuable rarities include certain Cape of Good Hope triangulars, the 1851 Hawaiian 'missionaries', the Austrian Mercury heads, Moldavia 'bulls', and some early Swiss canton stamps.

The rare 1-cent British Guiana reproduced on a Guyana commemorative issue in 1967

Penny Black commemorative

Brazilian 'bull's eye' centenary issue

Mauritius 'Post Office' Twopence Blue reproduced on the centenary stamp

'Zurich numeral' and 'Double Geneva' commemorative, 1968

One Penny Cape triangular. Centenary issue

Even the rare ones can be collected as 'stamps on stamps'

The collector's dictionary

Left: perforation and margin tab

Above: town and date mark

Adhesive stamp. One that has to be stuck directly on to a letter by the sender.

A.P.O. Army Post Office.

Backstamps. Stamps and marks on the back of the envelope, often showing the route the letter has taken.

Bantams. Miniature stamps issued by South Africa during World War II to save paper.

Bisects. Half stamps. From time to time some countries have allowed half stamps to be used when normal stamps were in short supply.

Block. Four or more stamps still joined together (two up and two down) by the original perforations.

Cancellation. The mark officially put on a stamp to prevent its re-use.

Charity stamps. Some countries issue stamps on which there is a small extra charge to be paid to charity. The charity sum is usually printed alongside the actual postal value, with a + sign separating them.

Commemoratives. Stamps marking a special occasion. A separate section is given to them on page 23.

Cover. The whole stamped envelope exactly as it comes through the post. There is more about them on page 20.

Definitive stamps. 'Regular' issues for use over a long and indefinite period. (*See* page 23.)

Slogan postmark

Watermark

Coil stamp

Overprints: V for victory, Somalia use of British stamp, and an 'official use'

A pair of bantams

Perfin

Killer obliteration

Postage due stamps from Holland and Monaco

Embossed stamp. One that is made by stamping the design in relief, giving a raised look.

Face value. The price actually printed on the stamp.

Fake. A stamp that has been altered to deceive a collector.

F.D.C. First day cover.

F.P.O. Field Post Office, an army post office dealing with letters posted by troops on active service.

Forgery. A copy of a stamp made to deceive collectors and authorities.

Frank. A stamp that shows a letter is to be carried free. Soldiers on active service, prisoners of war and some government departments may have the right to send franked mail.

Killer. A heavy cancellation mark which 'kills' the stamp underneath to prevent re-use.

Locals. Stamps valid for use only within a limited area of a country.

Maximum card. Called the maxi card for short. This is a picture postcard with 'matching' stamp, picture and postmark. For example, a stamp depicting a famous person affixed to a picture postcard of that person and postmarked in the place of his birth or death or with a commemorative postmark is a maxi card.

Meter mark. A mark stamped by machine directly on to an envelope or a gummed slip to show that postage has been paid although no stamp is affixed.

Mint stamp. An unused stamp in absolutely perfect condition. Even the gum must be unused and uncracked.

Newspaper stamp. Early stamps issued first as a tax on newspapers, and later to show special postage rates on them.

Obsolete stamp. No longer on sale.

Official. Stamps used by government departments. Sometimes they are of special design and sometimes they are regular stamps overprinted to show their official use.

Omnibus issue. Some events are of worldwide interest and become the subjects of commemorative issues in more than one country. For example, the Olympic Games are always commemorated in most of the countries taking part. The result is an omnibus issue.

Overprint. Words or figures officially added to a stamp after printing to alter it in some way, perhaps to show use abroad, or official use.

Pair. Two stamps joined together by the original perforation, either vertically or horizontally.

Perfin. A stamp punched with tiny holes forming

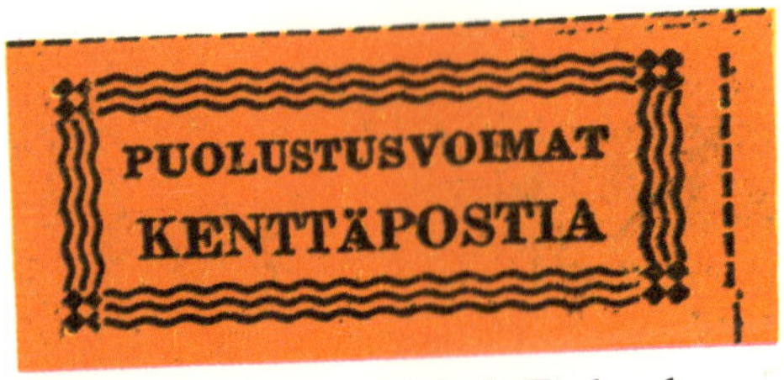

Military field post label, Finland

A charity stamp, Netherlands

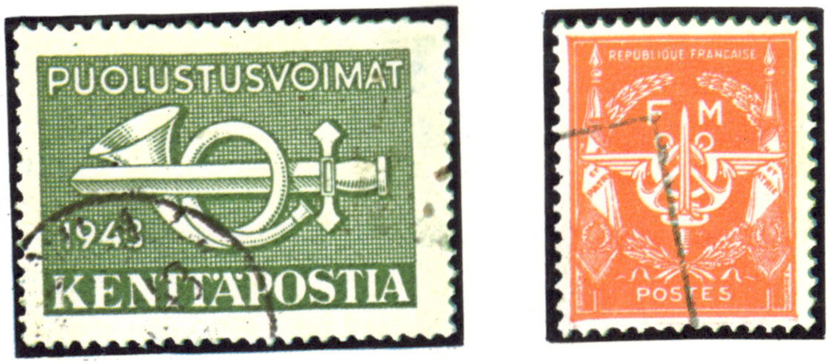

Military franks from Finland and France

Italian parcel stamp, the left half to put on the parcel, the right half to be kept as a receipt

Express stamp, Italy

Official stamp, Norway

initials or some other symbol to identify the user.

Perforation. The holes punched round the edges of stamps to allow them to be separated easily. Another method of separation is by rouletting a pattern of tiny cuts in the paper.

Postage due stamps. Special stamps added to a letter by the post office when the sender has not paid enough postage. The sum due is then collected from the receiver.

Postal stationery. Stationery items (postal cards, letter cards, aerogrammes, etc.) that have been pre-printed by the postal authorities ready for use.

Postmark. Any mark put on a letter by a postal service whether it cancels the stamp or not.

Pre-cancels. Stamps specially cancelled *before* they pass through the mails. Many countries offer a special pre-cancel service to ensure that collectors get clear postmarks. But such stamps are not highly valued.

R.P.O. Railroad Post Office. A travelling post office attached to a train.

Mobile post office mark

Registered mail label
and airmail etiquette

A tied stamp

Meter marks

An embossed stamp

Above: a German 'Europa' issue
Left: a United Nations stamp

Set. A complete series of all the stamps of one issue.

Se-tenant. Two or more stamps of different design or value or colour joined together.

Strip. Three or more stamps in a row still joined by the original perforations.

Surcharge. An overprint to show a change in face value.

Tied cover. When the postmark is stamped partly over the stamp and partly over the envelope the stamp is said to be *tied* to the cover.

T.P.O. Travelling post office. It may be a whole train or part of a train fitted out to deal with mail. It may even be on board ship.

Used and unused. A used stamp is a cancelled stamp. But an unused stamp is not necessarily a *mint* stamp.

Watermark. An identifying mark built into the paper the stamp is printed on to prevent forgeries. There are several ways of detecting watermarks. Some can be seen simply by holding the stamp to the light at a certain angle, others by damping very lightly with water or benzine as shown on page 13. Be sure to seek the advice of an experienced collector before applying benzine to *any* stamp as the paper and ink used for some stamps are damaged by benzine.

A se-tenant pair: two adjoining stamps of different designs

A block of stamps: four or more joined together by the original horizontal and vertical perforations

A strip of stamps: three or more joined by the original perforations. They may be in a horizontal strip, as here, or a vertical strip

Equipment and arranging

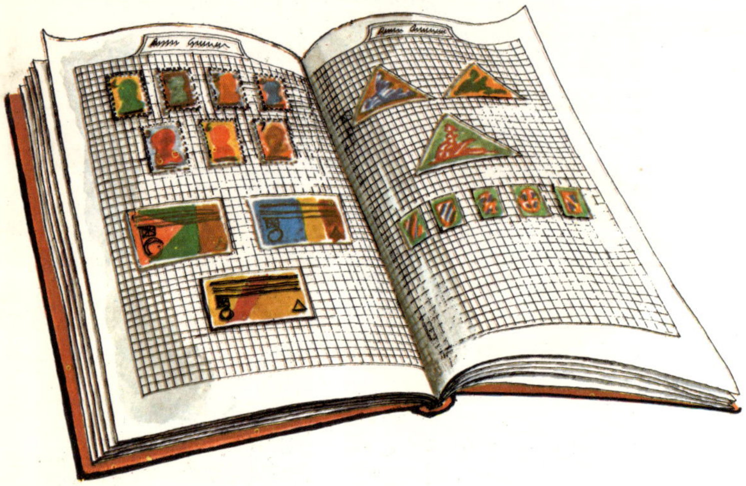

THE ALBUM

The best album for a new collector is one that gives a page for each country but leaves you free to arrange your collection on the page as you wish. Such albums are usually quadrillé, that is, printed with tiny squares to help position the stamps neatly.

Once you are sure that collecting is going to be a long-term hobby, buy a loose-leaf album printed on one side only. Pages can then be added whenever and wherever needed – and rearranged as required.

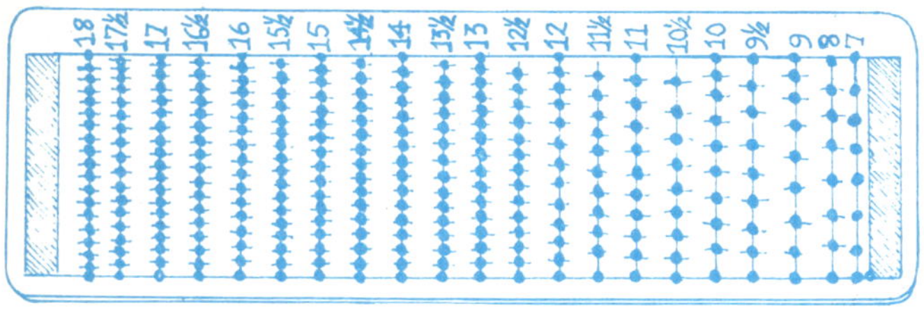

A simple perforation gauge

PERFORATION GAUGE

There are many different sizes and shapes of perforation hole. A perforation gauge measures the number of holes in any 2-centimetre length of stamp. Simply match it against the stamp until you find the perforation that fits. If there are 12 perforation holes to each two centimetres the stamp is Perf 12, as the experts say. If there are 10, then it is Perf 10, and so on. Measure both the horizontal and the vertical sides. If one is Perf 12 and the other Perf 14, the stamp is said to be Perf 12 × 14. The top measurement is always given first, then the side measurement.

Fixing hinges: 1. Moisten small folded part of hinge. 2. Fix to back of stamp just below the top perforation and allow to dry. 3. Moisten *bottom* edge of hinge and fix the stamp in the album.

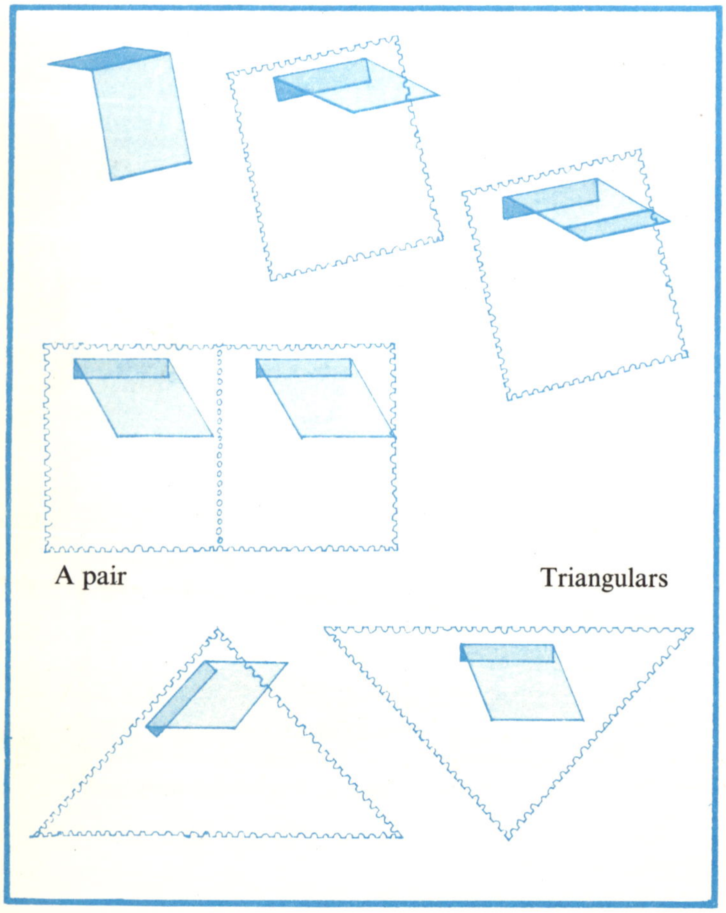

CATALOGUE

An illustrated stamp catalogue, arranged country by country in date of issue order, is the best help in identifying the stamps you already have and also those still needed to complete a set.

STAMP HINGES

Never mount a stamp with its own gum. Use good quality hinges which will peel off easily later without damaging the stamps. The drawings show where to place the hinges on stamps of different shapes.

To peel old hinges, soften them with a slightly damp painting brush and gently ease from the stamp. Then allow to dry slowly between sheets of blotting paper.

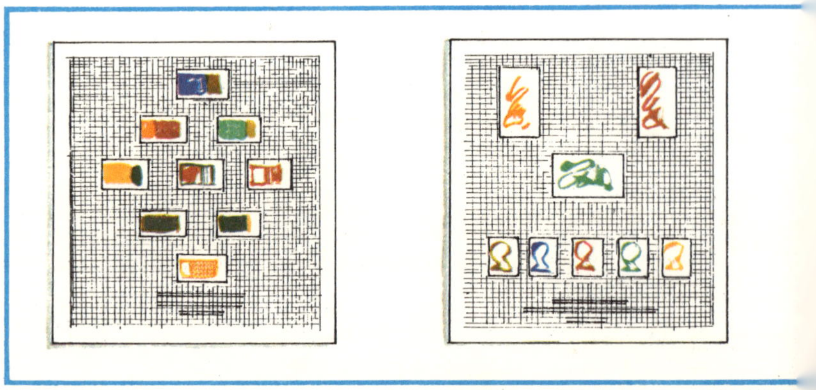

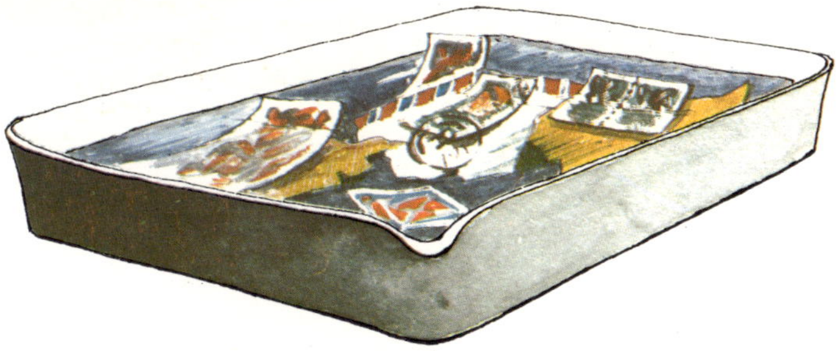

Soften the gum by floating the stamp face upwards in a shallow dish of water for 10 to 15 minutes. With the stamp face down on clean blotting paper peel the paper from the back. Make sure that all the gum has been washed away, then allow to dry slowly.

STOCK BOOK

A small stock book with transparent pockets protects the stamps until you are ready to mount or swap them.

BOWL AND BLOTTING PAPER

Both are very vital to every collector who has to remove paper sticking to a stamp.

The technique is to float the stamps face upwards in a shallow bowl of water for 10 minutes or so and then peel the paper from the stamp, not the stamp from the paper. And *never* when the paper is dry.

TWEEZERS

Use round-ended tweezers or tongs whenever you handle the stamps. Fingers damage them no matter how careful you think you are.

MAGNIFYING GLASS

This is valuable for reading small inscriptions and for examining printing details when you are more expert.

HOW TO GROUP THE STAMPS

If you are following a country-by-country arrangement, mount the stamps issue by issue, year by year with spaces left for those you have still to get. Make separate groups for definitives, commemoratives, airmails, postage due and official stamps, and special stamps like Christmas or charity sets.

Mint stamps look better if they are mounted separately, apart from the used stamps.

Even if your collection is arranged by topics, you still need system in the arrangement. For example, if you are an animal stamp collector, group them by the continents they come from, or by their type.

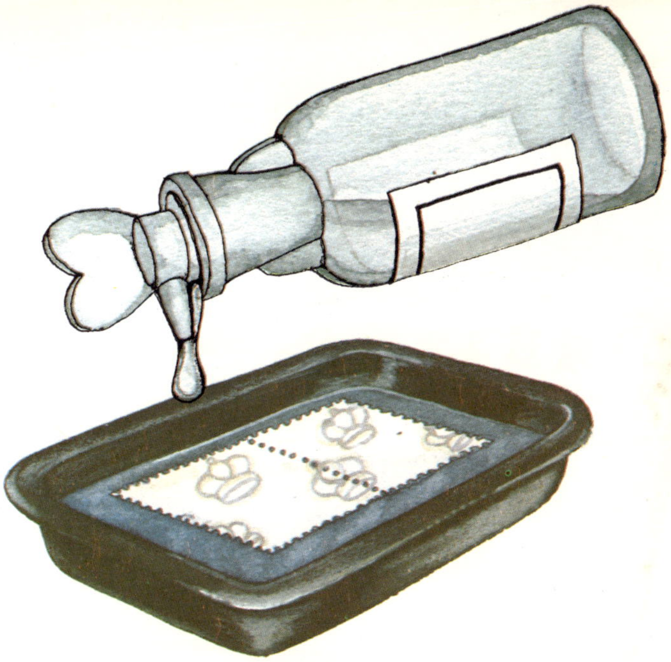

A tiny drop of water or benzine on the back of a stamp laid in a watermark detecting tray or on a black tile surface will reveal stubborn watermarks. But seek the advice of an experienced collector before applying benzine to *any* stamp because some inks and papers can be damaged by it. And always keep well away from any flame as benzine is inflammable.

PAGE ARRANGEMENTS

There are many ways of setting the stamps out in a looseleaf album and much depends on the collector's fancy. But usually the simpler layouts look best.

There are many pleasing arrangement patterns: pyramids, upside-down pyramids, diamonds, and of course the straight-line arrangement.

Overcrowded pages are unattractive. So is a top heavy or bottom heavy look. Space should be left for any notes you want to add.

Where you can, line up the tops of your stamps.

Move them about and try several arrangements before finally mounting them. When you have decided on the pattern, pencil lightly round each stamp. Remove them and pencil in your notes. Ink the notes over *and let them dry*. Then mount the stamps and remove the pencil outlines with a very soft rubber.

Short notes and simple headings show the stamps off to best effect. Fussy coloured headings and long notes overpower them.

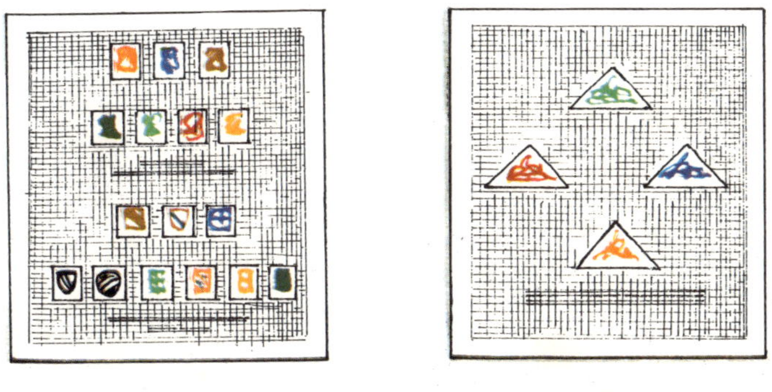

In a loose-leaf album stamps can be arranged in many ways. The secret of a good-looking collection is to keep it simple, as shown here.

Choosing what to collect

Locomotives and railroads

Motor vehicles of past and present

Sports and sporting events

Life and customs in other lands

Space exploration

Stamp collecting is one of the rare hobbies without fixed rules. Except for a few dos and donts about handling the stamps you are fairly free to make your own. You can collect what you fancy and arrange your collection as you please, though some methods are better than others.

Torn, dirty or damaged stamps should be avoided. Well centred stamps (with even margins all round) and fairly light but clear cancellations are the best. And a small collection built up into complete sets is likely to be worth more than a hotch-potch.

Most people begin by being general collectors. But as almost six thousand new stamps are issued every year, no modern collector can hope to make even a reasonably complete whole-world collection. One solution is to make a one-country collection, starting with current issues and building up complete sets, filling in the older sets as the budget allows. Another solution is to collect a particular topic.

WHAT TO SPECIALISE IN

The stamps of your own country? Although high prices for rare stamps will prevent you from making a *complete* collection, you will quickly have an impressive range to which new issues can be added as they come along.

If you have friends living abroad, you could do worse than specialise in 'their' country.

TOPIC COLLECTING

More and more collectors are abandoning the country-by-country arrangement and are collecting by themes or topics instead.

The choice of topics is wide: birds, animals, flags, important events in history, scientific inventions, trains, automobiles, costume, sport, space flight, exploration and discovery.

It is difficult to think of a subject that could not be collected.

You may later decide to specialise in one class of stamp: definitives, commemoratives, airmails, special stamps or Christmas stamps.

SOURCE OF SUPPLY

The beginner's first question is always the same: where will I get stamps from? First, there are family letters. And there are friends, especially if they were once collectors themselves. But the beginner's richest source is the mixed packet sold cheaply in most countries. They contain plenty of interesting material to get a collection moving.

Right: the animal kingdom is a very popular topic to collect

BRITTLE STAR
35 cents
BARBADOS
CRANA
Tilapia mossambica
EIIR
1/2 cent
BRITISH HONDURAS
CANADA
15 CENTS
POSTES POSTAGE
CERATOTHERIUM SIMUM
20c
BELGISCH CONGO BELGE
RUANDA
GORILLA
10c
URUNDI
CORREOS
ZORZAL
2c
URUGUAY
IMP. NACIONAL
5c
CONUS MARMOREUS
PAPUA & NEW GUINEA
LIBAN
لبنان
POSTE AERIENNE
40P.
VULCAIN
NOUVELLE CALEDONIE
ET DEPENDANCES
POSTES
RF
40c
JULES DOUY DEL.
KAGOUS
H-V PARIS
HERMIT CRAB
9c
AUSTRALIA
中國人民郵政
REPUBLIQUE FEDERALE DU CAMEROUN
CERCOPITHEQUE MOUSTAC
0F50
POSTES
5 Cts
SAHARA ESPAÑOL
DIA DEL SELLO COLONIAL 1955
CORREOS

Where does it come from?

12-pointed sun symbol: China

Chrysanthemum motif: Japan

Letters looking like CH at the beginning of the inscription: South Korea

Shqiperise: Albania

Hellas: Greece

CCCP: Russia

The Cyrillic letters printed below the train spell out the name 'Bulgaria'

Since most countries follow the Universal Postal Union's recommendation to print their names on each stamp issue, it is not usually difficult to identify the source of modern stamps – once the collector has learned to recognise each country's name in its own language. Many are the same as or very similar to their English equivalents (Portugal, Danmark, Nederland). Others are close enough to be recognisable: Espana (Spain), Norge (Norway), Belgique (Belgium). Some inscriptions are less obvious but are quickly learned, like Österreich (Austria), Helvetia (Switzerland), Sverige (Sweden), Nippon (Japan).

The inscriptions of the major issuing countries are given in this book, and an illustrated catalogue will provide many more.

Older stamps are the ones most likely to give trouble. With these, sometimes the postmark or the currency shown by the face value can help to pinpoint the origin. And sometimes a national emblem offers the needed clue. For example, a twelve-pointed sun symbol was used on Chinese stamps between 1931 and 1943. Japanese stamps carried a small chrysanthemum motif for many years. A palm tree with crossed swords was used by Saudi Arabia, and a crescent with a star above it by Turkey.

Unfamiliar foreign alphabets such as Chinese, Japanese, Arabic, Hebrew, Greek or Cyrillic (the alphabet used on Russian, Bulgarian and some Yugoslavian stamps) are also problem-makers. But again, the collector soon learns to recognise the 'shape' of each alphabet, even if the meaning of the words remains a mystery. At least the shape of the country's name becomes familiar in most cases. For example, after studying the Cyrillic characters for the name 'Bulgaria' printed under the train design opposite, it is an easy matter to identify other Bulgarian stamps with the same inscription.

After deciding the basic group of a 'foreign alphabet' stamp (Oriental, Arabic, Cyrillic and so on) the origin can be traced with the aid of a good catalogue.

Once the origin is known, it is necessary to decide what *kind* of stamp it is. The main classes you will encounter are definitive, commemorative, airmail, postage due, officials, military frank, parcel, special delivery and charity stamps. It is practical to make a list of foreign words used to indicate these classes. *Par avion, flugpost, lugpos, luchtpost, flygpost, posta aerea* and *correos aereos* are some of the words meaning airmail. While *te betalen, timbre taxe, à percevoir, portomarke* and *segnatasse* are some of those used on postage due stamps.

Strange shapes

Cola nut 'free shape'.
Sierra Leone

Many collectors have a soft spot for oddball shapes. Some even make a special study of them.

The first triangular was issued by the Cape of Good Hope in 1853. One of the hobby's most spectacular stories centres around Cape triangulars. In 1863 two sailors walked into the Plymouth shop of the father of a young man called Stanley Gibbons, later to become the famous dealer. The young man could hardly believe his ears when for £5 they offered him a kit-bag full of Cape stamps, with many triangulars among them. They had won them in a raffle while ashore in Cape Province. Today Cape triangulars rate among the world's classics.

The first star shape was produced by Colombia in 1865, and the first shield shape by Argentina in 1867. The first circular stamp came from the Roman States in 1852 and the first diamond shape from the Somali Coast in 1894.

There have since been many variations on these geometrical designs, and recently many 'free shapes' have made their appearance. But the prize must surely go to Tonga for the world's first – and doubtless last – banana-shaped stamp. Because perforation would be difficult with such a shape, the 'bananas' are sold with sticky backing paper to be peeled off before use.

Tonga has also produced a map-of-the-island stamp, as well as big metal foil discs representing its coins.

Sierra Leone has contributed a cola nut shape, and Gibraltar a stamp perforated in the shape of the Rock itself. Malta's five-sided stamp, shown here, was ingeniously designed to allow the stamps to be printed and perforated in sheet form. Try working out how they fit together!

Serious collectors frown on these frivolous shapes, and they may be right to disapprove – but the shapes have a curiosity value and add a touch of humour to any album.

Five-sided perforated stamp. Malta

Free-shape self-adhesive 'banana' stamp. Tonga

Triangular postage due stamp, Monaco

Perforated 'Rock' shape. Gibraltar

Diamond shape. Niger

Above: an American FDC franked with the first Stars and Stripes and the Bunker Hill flag, two of the ten 'Historic Flag' designs.

Below: a souvenir cover for the fiftieth anniversary of the first two-way air crossing of the Atlantic Ocean in 1919 by airship R34.

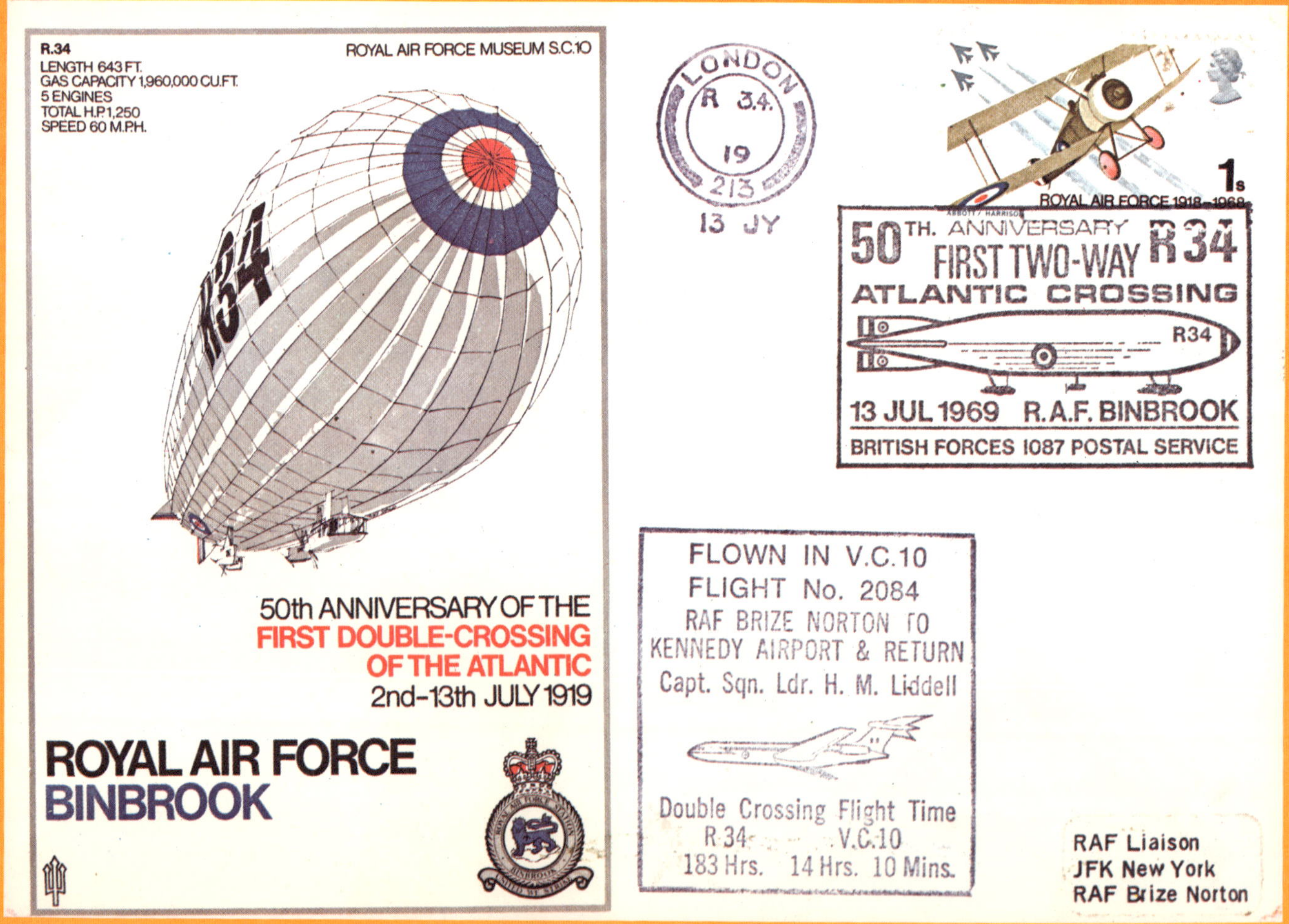

What is a postmark?

Paquebot mark (*left*) and a souvenir cachet (*right*) commemorating the death of the airship pioneer Graf von Zeppelin.

A postmark is *any* postal mark put on a letter during its journey through the mails and has quite a lot to tell a collector.

A *townmark* shows where a letter was posted, often helping to identify difficult foreign stamps quickly.

A *date stamp* shows the date of posting. This too can be useful to the collector. It may prove whether a cover is a first day cover or not.

Sometimes the date and townmark are combined in a single mark.

There are also many special postmarks to show that letters have been posted at sea, on a train, in a late fee box, at a railway station or from a military field post.

There are postmarks for letters posted from the top of some high mountain passes. There has even been a postmark from the bottom of the sea, and another from a submarine under the North Pole, and souvenir postmarks are often used at important exhibitions and other events.

First day covers often have special postmarks. For example, American FDCs to commemorate the 1969 moon landing were postmarked 'moon landing'.

A *cancellation mark* is a postmark which defaces a stamp so that it can't be used again. The first cancellations were simply pen marks. Then came handstamp cancellations: there were circles, ovals, diamonds and so on, some with very heavy 'killer' bars and some with numbers built into the design to identify the post office from which the letter had been sent.

Later, duplex cancellations were devised to date and cancel with a single handstamp. Finally, as the world's mails grew bigger, handstamping took too long and automatic cancelling machines took over.

Collecting postmarks. Look for clear, unsmudged impressions, and keep any envelope with especially interesting markings intact.

Other postmarks which you may want to keep for general interest are best cut to a standard size (4 inches long by 2 inches deep is practical) and then 'filed' in a shallow cardboard box to protect them.

Just as some collectors collect topic stamps, so others collect topic postmarks – capital cities, the names of famous people (Wellington, Washington, Nelson) or just odd-sounding places (Middle Wallop, Moose Jaw, Wagga Wagga).

Finnish ship's mark

Airmail mark

Route mark

Special mark for the first moon landing

Vatican City postmark

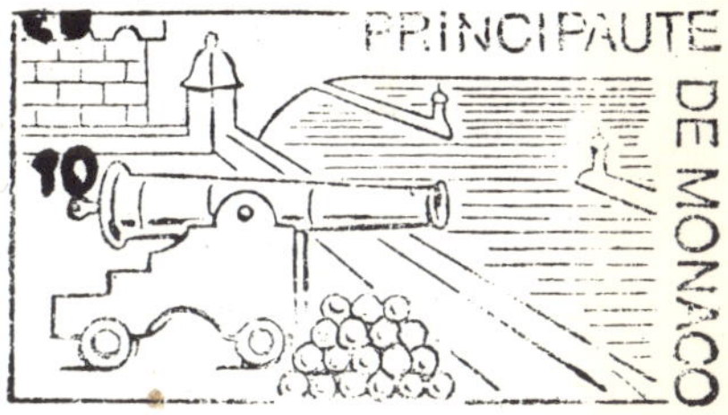

Slogan postmark

First-day-of-issue mark on a Christmas aerogramme.
By courtesy of the British Postal Museum

Covers: what to look for

A 1929 catapult cover, carried by a hydroplane catapulted from the deck of a German ship, *Karlsruhe*, to the coast of Ireland. *By courtesy of Francis F. Field*

A valuable *first flight cover* carried by airship *Graf Zeppelin* on a flight from the U.S.A. to Friedrichshafen, Germany. *By courtesy of Francis F. Field*

A *bisect* cover franked with a 25 cent stamp halved diagonally and used to prepay 12½ centimes of the postage from Cuba to Marseilles via New York and London, 1875. *By courtesy of Walter Hubbard*

A *paquebot cover* posted at sea in a Cunard liner in 1896. The TPO mark was added by a travelling post office aboard the train carrying mails from the port of arrival. *By courtesy of Alan Robertson*

A *cover* is the whole envelope or wrapper exactly as it went through the mails. The combination of stamp, postmark, cancellation and any other official mark put on the envelope during its journey may be valuable. So look carefully before stripping stamps off their covers.

It is unlikely that you will want to specialise in cover collecting at first, but have at least one or two. And post FDCs to yourself whenever you can.

Covers can be mounted with triangular corner mounts or in a special cover album with protective transparent sleeves to hold them.

FDCs
These are first day covers carrying new stamp issues postmarked with the first day of issue. They should carry the full set of the new issue and must actually go through the mails to be of value.

FIRST FLIGHT COVERS
These are the covers carried on the first flight of a new air route. Many of the early ones are now very valuable.

From time to time special flights are made to commemorate the pioneer flights, and covers like the one shown on page 18 are carried and given special cancellations or cachets. Although some collectors look on them as valueless because they are not 'proper' postal items, they add a lot of interest to an album.

MARITIME COVERS
Letters posted at sea may carry the stamps of one country and the postmarks of another. To explain this they have an additional postmark, often incorporating the word *paquebot* (packet ship) or a foreign equivalent. They may also have markings to show the name of the ship and its tonnage. Older seaborne letters may carry the mark 'ship letter'.

WRECK COVERS
When a ship is wrecked or an aircraft crashes, mail on board is given special markings to explain the delay and damage. And if the letters arrive in an 'ambulance' (a post office cover), this should be mounted beside the original cover.

AIRMAIL COVERS
Look for special airmail stamps and the many airmail labels or etiquettes. The etiquettes have no real philatelic value but are interesting in a general way.

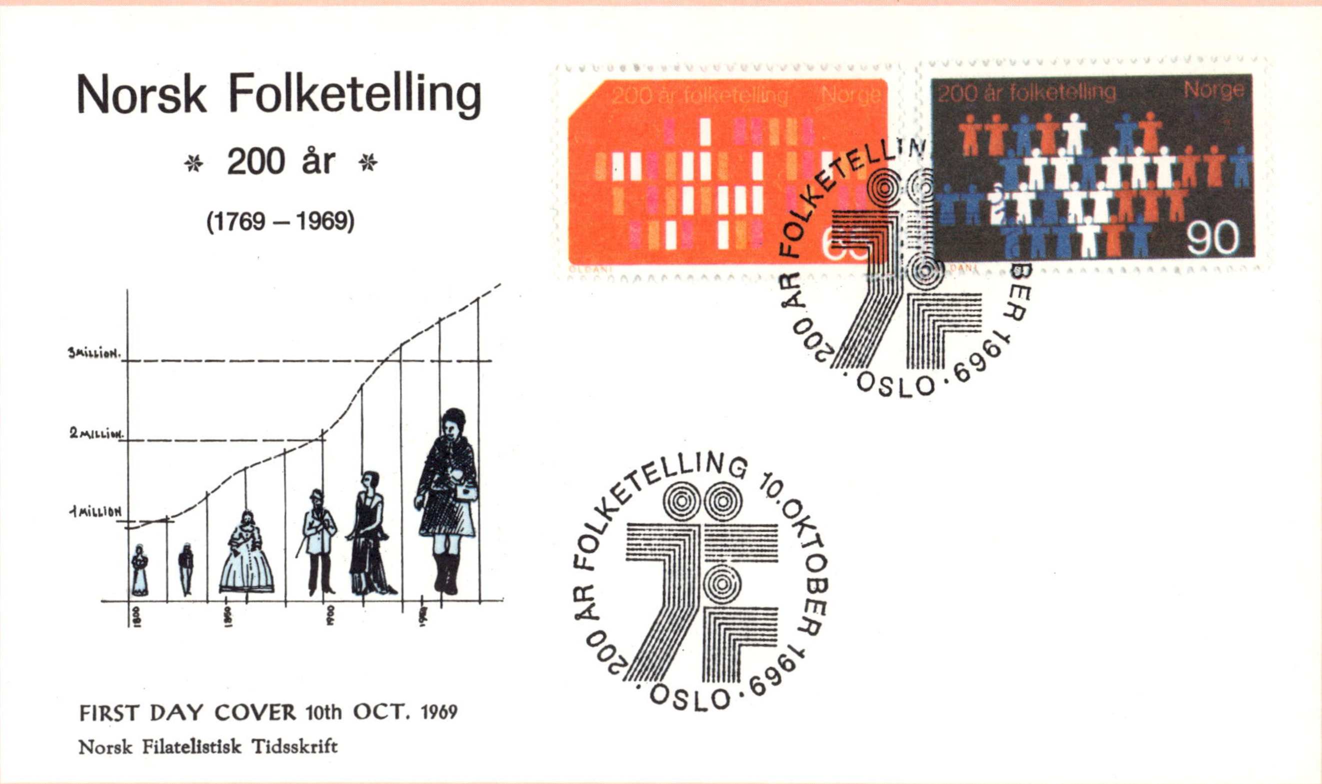

Above: a precancelled Norwegian first day cover commemorating the national census. Although the stamps are officially cancelled, the envelope has not been postally used.

Below: backstamps on a 1969 souvenir cover to commemorate the first England-to-Australia flight in 1919.

Portraits of the head of state and symbolic designs are familiar definitive themes

Coats of arms are also common

Numeral designs are frequently used on definitives too

Small pictorial types have gradually replaced earlier definitives in many countries

Definitives and commemoratives

Stamps issued to do regular postal service over a long period are called definitives. They are usually long sets, often with identical or similar designs for the entire range of values needed for all postal purposes: cards, letters, parcels and so on.

Designs of modern definitives are varied and often pictorial. But older ones usually show the reigning monarch's head, the national coat of arms, a national symbol, or a plain numeral design.

It is not unknown for a country to select a design for a definitive issue and go on using it for over fifty years or more. The Sudan's camel postman design is a good example. It was used from 1898 until after World War II.

Although the basic designs of definitives remain unchanged for long periods, there are many variations to collect over the years. Changes in the watermarks, the colours, the perforations, face values and so on are all collectable.

When designs are printed over and over again the printing plates become worn and have to be replaced. This leads to slight differences between printings from one plate and printings from another. Expert collectors take great satisfaction in identifying and collecting the different 'platings'.

Sometimes changes are made in the colours. For example, in 1969 Britain's low value $\frac{1}{2}$d red was discontinued because it no longer had any postal value. The red was then used for the 4d stamp because the automatic sorting devices had difficulty with its original colour.

Face values of definitives may sometimes be changed. For example, the face value of the stamps of Australia, New Zealand and Great Britain had to be changed when they introduced decimal currency.

Collecting full sets of definitives can be quite expensive. Many collectors therefore limit themselves to what are called 'short sets', omitting the high values. Others 'specialise' in a particular denomination, collecting all the different stamps of that value ever issued as definitives.

COMMEMORATIVES
These are special stamps issued to celebrate centenaries, coronations, royal weddings, space flights, big sporting events, independence days, anniversaries of famous events or discoveries and the like. They are usually printed in limited numbers and are best collected on first day covers if possible.

Denmark: royal wedding

Germany: John Kennedy memorial stamp

Canada: opening of the Trans-Canada Highway

U.S.A : baseball centenary

Italy: the death of St Francis

Great Britain

Ireland

The Penny Black
From the Reginald M. Phillips Collection by courtesy of the National Postal Museum

Victorian penny lilac

A first bi-colour

Edward VII

George V

Edward VIII

George VI

Elizabeth II

Decimal issue, 1971

Britain's stamp history began with the world's first adhesive stamps, the Penny Black and the Twopence Blue of 1840. They were beautifully engraved with a portrait of Queen Victoria, a portrait the Queen liked so much that it was used during the whole sixty years of her reign.

The first stamps were imperforate and had to be cut from their sheets with scissors. This was a slow business. A quicker and neater method of separation was later devised: perforation. This involved punching tiny holes from the paper round the edge of each stamp.

In 1847 Britain produced the world's first embossed stamp, and in 1854 the world's first perforated stamps, the popular Penny Reds.

The most colourful Victorian issues were the 'Jubilee' stamps of 1887, Britain's first two-colour issue. Their style and colours were also used for most of the Edward VII issues.

For forty years the monarch's head was the almost unchanging main motif right through the reigns of Edward VII, George V, Edward VIII and George VI.

The head of the uncrowned Edward VIII appears on just four stamps, all issued in 1936 and all showing the crown set to one side of the stamp instead of immediately above the monarch's head.

The first British commemorative was issued for the British Empire Exhibition in 1924 and 1925. But it was not until the reign of the present queen that British stamps really blossomed with popular themes and new designs. Many collectors now stick to collecting 'Elizabeth IIs' only – and they are kept pretty busy. Shakespeare, Charles Dickens, Sir Winston Churchill, Concorde's first flight, the *Mayflower*, Captain Cook, the Battle of Britain, flowers, cathedrals and famous paintings are just a few of the subjects issued.

Not only are there many new designs but also a new currency. In 1971 Britain introduced a new decimal coinage with one hundred new pence to the pound.

Scotland, Wales, Northern Ireland and the Isle of Man issue regional stamps in certain face values, with designs closely resembling British definitives but with a thistle and St Andrew's Cross for Scotland (until 1971), a dragon for Wales, a gloved hand for Northern Ireland, and a three-legged symbol for the Isle of Man. Jersey and Guernsey have had their own issues since 1969.

First stamp issued: 1840
Currency: 100 new pence (100p)=£1
until 1971 12 pence (12d)=1 shilling
Inscription: Postage Revenue

Regional stamps from Scotland, Northern Ireland and Wales

Eire has its own stamps

Silver wedding of King George VI

Battle of Britain commemorative

The hovercraft

World Cup winners, 1966

A Norman ship, one of a set commemorating the Norman invasion of Britain in 1066

Round-the-world yacht *Gypsy Moth IV*

The world's largest steerable radio telescope at Jodrell Bank

Dickens' centenary stamp: Mr Pickwick

The Post Office Tower, London

Australia

The first all-Australia design (*left*) and Australia's first royal portrait type

The world's first pictorial stamp was a view of Sydney taken from the colonial seal of New South Wales in 1851. It was also the first stamp issued in Australia.

The other states followed quickly – Queensland, Tasmania, South Australia and Victoria with portrait stamps of Queen Victoria, and Western Australia with the most famous state stamp of them all, the black swan design. Its fame came partly from a printing error which had the final effect of making the swan look as if it was swimming upside down.

When the six states united in 1901 to form the Commonwealth of Australia, each went on issuing its own stamps until 1913, when the first all-Australia stamp was issued. It was the now-familiar kangaroo and map design. Then came numerous George V heads.

Although there have been many fine portrait stamps of reigning monarchs the best-known Australian portrait stamp is not of a king or a queen but of One Pound Jimmy, an aborigine whose tribal name was Gwoja Jungarai. He had earned his nickname very simply. Whenever he was asked how much he wanted for doing a job, he would reply 'One pound, boss'.

Animal definitives: koala, bandicoot, emu and platypus

Until 1966 face values were in shillings and pence. From then on, the year in which Australia went decimal, they are in Australian dollars and cents.

Because Australia was for thousands of years an isolated continent, it has many animals and birds not found anywhere else in the world. Some of them appear in stamp designs, including the kangaroo, the koala bear and the platypus, a unique mammal that lays eggs. And the emu, which – like New Zealand's kiwi – belongs to a group of birds called ratites which have lost the power of flight.

One Pound Jimmy

Queen Elizabeth II

The six state floral emblems can be collected in the 1968 definitive series: the kangaroo paw (Western Australia), the pink heath (Victoria), the Tasmanian Blue Gum (Tasmania), Sturt's Desert Pea (Southern Australia), the Cooktown Orchid (Queensland), and the waratah (New South Wales).

An interesting set of famous navigators issued in 1963 (and again in 1966 with decimal values) includes Cook, Tasman, Flinders, Dampier, Bass and King, each with the ship he sailed in.

Antarctic exploration features strongly on the stamps with survey teams at work, penguins, dog teams, icebergs and snowtrack vehicles.

Two decimal definitives

First stamp issued: 1913 (first state stamp 1851)
Currency: 100 cents = 1 Australian dollar
Inscription: Australia

Four state 'firsts' on centenary issues: Western Australia, New South Wales, Victoria and South Australia

Cobb's coaches (*above*) were official carriers of early Australian mails. Mounted postmen and mail planes (*below*) came later.

Christmas issues: The Three Wise Men, and the Adoration of the Shepherds

Explorers crossing the Blue Mountains

The Overlanders

Remote districts rely on the flying doctor service

Matthew Flinders and his ship *Investigator*. *Left:* William Dampier and *Roebuck*.

Shackleton's expedition at the South Magnetic Pole

New Zealand

Kiwi definitive

Fantail

George V in marshal's (not admiral's) uniform

Old and new currency values on the kowhai design

The arrival of the Maori

Left: a health stamp with a morse message
Right: lamb, a major export

A Dutchman, Abel Tasman, discovered New Zealand in 1642 and named it after Zeeland, a province in Holland. But it was Captain James Cook who discovered that there were two islands, North Island and South Island, and in 1840 both became British territory.

Like many Commonwealth countries, New Zealand chose a portrait of Queen Victoria for her first stamps. Then came a succession of different 'queen's head' designs until the first pictorials of 1898 showed Mount Cook (New Zealand's highest mountain), Lake Wakatipu (spelled Wakitipu on the first stamps and later corrected), and the kea and the kiwi, two New Zealand birds.

Health stamps, 'admirals' and 'Anzacs' are New Zealand stamps that collectors soon learn to recognise. The 'admirals' are portraits of King George V in the full dress uniform of an admiral of the fleet. Beware of wrongly identifying the George V field-marshal portrait as an 'admiral'. The field marshal's hat is the plumed, ornate one.

The health stamps have been issued every year since 1930 and carry a surcharge to provide money for children's health camps. They have fitting designs such as the Peter Pan statue in London, Boy Scouts and Girl Guides, and young rugger and cricket players.

The Anzac Day stamps commemorate the landing of Australian and New Zealand soldiers at Gallipoli on April 25 1915 during World War I.

Many of New Zealand's strange-sounding place, plant and bird names are of Maori origin. Examples found on stamps include the kotuku, the kakariki, and the poaka (all birds), and the titoki, the kowhai and the pikiarero (flowers and plants).

The Maoris are native New Zealanders who fought fiercely to try to keep their land and their independence when the white settlers first arrived. Maori subjects featured on New Zealand stamps include a council meeting, a rock drawing, a letter carrier, a tiki or sacred amulet, and a Maori Bible.

Ross Dependency is a New Zealand territory in Antarctica which issues its own stamps. Other dependent territories issuing stamps include several small Pacific islands: Niue, Tokelau Islands, Cook Islands (named after Captain James Cook), and the Samoan islands.

First stamp issued: 1855
Currency: 100 cents = 1 N.Z. dollar
Inscription: New Zealand

Canada

George V portrait type

'Beaver' centenary issue

Moose

2-cent definitive

There is a large French-speaking population in Canada and the inscription on the postage stamps is in French as well as English.

The first stamps of the 'colony of Canada' included the famous beaver design, a portrait of French explorer Jacques Cartier, Prince Albert, and three Queen Victoria values, including the now valuable 'Twelve Pence Black'. The words 'twelve pence' were used deliberately because at the time of issue twelve Canadian pence did *not* make a shilling everywhere in North America.

From 1859 onwards values are in cents and dollars.

Of the several provinces which issued their own stamps until the first 'dominion' issue in 1868, Newfoundland's are the most interesting. This province went on issuing its own stamps until 1949. By far the most exciting of them are the airmail overprints for the first attempts at carrying transatlantic mail between 1919 and 1923. Among the most valuable are the 'Hawker' covers for the first but unsuccessful flight in 1919. Almost 100 letters were carried, each with 'First Transatlantic Air Post' overprinted on the three-cent caribou stamp. But the flight crashed into the sea. Hawker, his crew and some of the mail were, happily, recovered. It was finally Alcock and Brown who made the first successful crossing later in 1919.

Stamps showing Queen Victoria usually portray her as a young queen, even at the end of her sixty-year reign. Canada, however, showed her as an elderly monarch. And for her diamond jubilee in 1897 there was a commemorative showing both a 'young head' and an 'old head' on the same stamp.

Like New Zealand, Canada has its 'admirals'. The difference is that the Canadian version shows King George bareheaded.

In a country as vast as Canada good road and rail routes are vital. It is not therefore surprising to find a stamp celebrating the opening of the Trans-Canada Highway in 1962, and another with a view of the Alaska Highway in the 1967 definitive series.

The Canadian prime minister series of 1951 and the provincial emblems of 1964 are well worth building up into complete sets. 'Singles' of special interest are a Canadian mountie (1935), a polar bear (1953), Canada geese (1963), a musk ox (1955), a totem pole (1967), skins drying outside Indian tepees (1950), an eskimo in a kayak (1953), and an early gold miner panning for gold (1958).

First stamp issued: 1851 (colony), 1868 (dominion)
Currency: 100 cents = 1 Canadian dollar
Inscription: Canada Postes-Postage

The Alaska Highway

Gold panning in British Columbia

The important codfish

The British Commonwealth

Map and flag of Jamaica

Commonwealth stamps are a good choice for a collector who wants to specialise but does not want a one-country collection. Thousands of definitives and commemoratives show lands of every continent, from the poles to the tropics, from the bare desert to the steamy jungle.

It is best to tackle one 'area' at a time. Perhaps Australia, New Zealand or Canada, each of which has a separate chapter in this book. Or one of the following smaller areas:

The British Virgin Islands

The West Indies should be represented by stamps from Jamaica, Trinidad, Tobago, Barbados, St Lucia, St Vincent, Grenada, Cayman, and Dominica. They produce brilliant pictorials of local industries, birds, carnivals and customs.

Also from the Caribbean area come the issues of Antigua, Barbuda, the Bahamas, Turks and Caicos, Bermuda, the tiny islands of St Kitts and Nevis, Montserrat, and the Virgin Islands.

St Lucia

Africa will add stamps from Botswana, Tanzania, Kenya, Uganda, the Gambia, Ghana, Lesotho, Malawi, Nigeria, Sierra Leone, Zambia, Zanzibar and South West Africa. Their stamps are described more fully on pages 48–51.

Commonwealth countries of the Far East include Brunei, Ceylon, Hong Kong, India, Malaysia, and Pakistan. Their stamps appear on pages 59–61.

Montserrat

Then there are the dozens of small islands. In the Indian Ocean there is Mauritius, the first British colony to issue stamps – in 1847. In the South Atlantic are the Falkland Islands, Tristan da Cunha, and South Georgia. And inside the polar circle lie the British Antarctic Territories.

Cyprus, Malta, Gibraltar, Ascension Island and St Helena, where Napoleon spent years of exile, also issue their own stamps. So does Guyana in South America and British Honduras in Central America.

But most exciting of all are the Pacific islands, with brilliant birds from Norfolk Island and Samoa, bright tropical flowers from Nauru, spear-fishing scenes from Fiji, war canoes from the British Solomon Islands, native dancers from the Gilbert and Ellice Islands. In Papua and New Guinea birds of paradise, butterflies and sea shells are common themes, while the story of Captain Bligh and the mutiny on the *Bounty* is shown on a Pitcairn Islands stamp. Tonga is now well known for its 'shape' stamps.

Barbados: file shell

Many Commonwealth countries have continued to incorporate the head of the ruling monarch in their designs even after their independence. Others have abandoned the monarch's portrait altogether.

Seychelles: sail fish

Mauritius: grey white-eye

Tristan da Cunha: crawfish

3-states issue: Mount Kenya

Botswana: ground-scraper thrush

Malawi: tea plantation

South Georgia: reindeer

British Antarctic: manhauling a load

Christmas Island

Fiji: spear fishing

Ceylon: tea picking

Solomon Islands: native canoes

Spain

Andorra

Like other early stamps, Spain's first issues were imperforate. They depicted the reigning queen, Isabella II, who curiously appears to grow younger and younger with each successive issue.

In the 1930s, while many countries were still printing stamps with simple designs, Spain began issuing fine pictorials.

In 1930 to celebrate the death centenary of Francisco Goya, one of the world's greatest artists, she issued stamps depicting both the painter and some of his paintings. One showed one of Goya's nude paintings and just as the original had shocked the public, so the stamp raised protests too.

Christopher Columbus, although Genoese by birth, had discovered the New World in the service of the King of Spain. In 1932 a set of pictorial stamps commemorated his epic voyage. Their life, however, was short. They came to a halt when the Civil War broke out in 1936.

Then followed years of poor stamp design, since in time of war it was not a matter of great importance.

After the Civil War, Spain became a republic and very slowly her stamps began to recover their reputation.

In the 1950s a style was introduced which has become very familiar, especially in the portraits of Spanish notables and religious themes.

In 1962 a series showing the coats of arms of the Spanish provinces introduced a new idea: it was to be issued at the rate of one new design every month. The designs and the method of issue proved to be so popular that the series continued until there were almost 60 different coats of arms.

Another long and equally colourful set began in 1967, again with the design-a-month method of issue. This time it showed gay provincial costumes.

Other recent and attractive series include tourist views and castles in Spain.

The stamps of the Spanish colonies and former colonies (Spanish Sahara, Ifni and Spanish Guinea) have designs very similar to those of Spain.

Andorra, a tiny state in the Pyrenees, perched between France and Spain, uses both French and Spanish post office stamps.

SPAIN	**First stamp issued: 1850** **Currency: 100 centimos = 1 peseta** **Inscription: Espana**
ANDORRA	**First stamp issued: 1928** **Currency: 100 centimos = 1 peseta** **100 centimes = 1 franc** **Inscription: Andorra, Andorre**

Queen Isabella II

General Franco

The *Santa Maria*, Columbus's ship

Castles: the Alcazar, Segovia

Costumes: Santander

Spanish Sahara: Stamp Day issue 1953

Andorra uses French *and* Spanish post office stamps

Portugal

Vasco da Gama's fleet

Ceres portrait type

Portugal's first stamp showed a cameo-type portrait head of Queen Maria. Then came other similar royal heads. A fine set of pictorials for the fourth centenary of Vasco da Gama's discovery of a sea route to India caught the attention of collectors as early as 1898. Some of these stamps can still be had for a shilling or two.

When the kingdom became a republic in 1910 the word 'Republica' was overprinted on king's head types. In 1920 the first of a very long series showing the goddess Ceres appeared. Counting the different values and colour changes, there are over 100 Ceres issues.

The 1926 set issued to celebrate the independence of Portugal was very popular. The stamps showed famous Portuguese soldiers and the battles they fought. They were issued for use on certain days instead of the usual definitives and the money from their sale was paid into a fund to buy a war museum.

It may seem strange to find the portrait of an Englishman on Portuguese stamps. But when the year of issue is 1940 and the man is Sir Rowland Hill, the reason is clear. The stamps celebrated the centenary of the first-ever adhesive stamp, which Sir Rowland had introduced to the world.

The Portuguese were once great navigators and made many famous voyages of discovery. Vasco da Gama, Bartholomew Diaz and Ferdinand Magellan all sailed in the service of the kings of Portugal.

The monarch who inspired and encouraged many of the most important voyages of discovery was Henry the Navigator, and he too has been commemorated on more than one stamp. Without him urging them on and putting ships at their disposal, many of the world's most famous discoverers might never have been known.

Wherever the Portuguese went they set up colonies and trading posts. Today, although only a strip of a country west of Spain, Portugal still has valuable overseas provinces. Among them are Portuguese Guinea, Angola, Cape Verde, Madeira, Mozambique Portuguese India, Timor (an island in the East Indies) and Macao, a busy trading port on the coast of China.

The overseas provinces issue stamps with strong pictorial designs closely resembling those of Portugal.

1926 Independence issue: the Battle of Aljubarrota

Early colonists in the Azores

Queen Maria cameo type on a stamp exhibition issue

Macao issue.

First stamp issued: 1853
Currency: 100 centavos = 1 escudo
Inscription: Republica Portuguesa, Portugal

Corn goddess Ceres and Napoleon III, the first French portrait subjects

The sower type (*left*) and Louis Pasteur (*right*)

The harvester (*left*) and a modern version of Marianne (*right*)

The Gallic cockerel, symbol of France

Coats of arms series: Oran and Paris

France

Monaco

The portraits of kings, queens and presidents have graced the definitive issues of most countries at some time or other, but France has always shown a strong preference for *symbolic* designs. Her first stamp, in 1849, showed the head of the corn goddess Ceres, a fitting symbol for a country with rich farm lands. Ceres has been redrawn and reissued many times since that first issue.

Other familiar figures are 'Peace and Commerce', 'the sower', 'the harvester' with sheaves of corn, 'Republie' with ears of wheat round her head, and the proud Gallic cockerel. And no self-respecting collection would be complete without at least one or two of the several 'Marianne' designs, the girl who is always portrayed wearing the bonnet of the French Revolutionaries. Like Ceres, Marianne has been redrawn more than once to bring her up to date.

Two real life personalities did, however, find their way on to French definitives: Napoleon III (nephew of Napoleon Bonaparte and Emperor of France), and Louis Pasteur the famous biologist.

But if French definitives lack real people, the pictorials and commemoratives more than make up for them with countless fine scenes from history, and dozens of generals, scientists, writers and musicians.

For those with an interest in postal history France has some fascinating Stamp Day designs, ranging from a Roman post coach to French postmen down the ages. And few collectors can resist the long and colourful coats of arms series. Or the many 'tourist publicity' stamps of beauty spots and famous buildings.

One of the most dramatic contributions to postal history was made by France during the siege of Paris in the Franco-Prussian War. In 1870 the beleagured city ingeniously flew mail right over the enemy Prussian lines by balloon post. And it was during this same siege that pigeon posts were used. The pigeons were flown out of Paris with the outgoing mail in the balloons, and released with reply communications at the end of the flight.

MONACO
Monaco is a tiny principality on the south coast of France with frequent issues of large and colourful pictorial stamps. Motor sport, ships and planes are typical themes. Face values are in French currency.

FRANCE **First stamp issued: 1849**
Currency: 100 centimes = 1 franc
Inscription: République Française, RF

Saint Louis, King of France, receiving the poor

Pierre Larousse

The gateway at Vire

Concorde's first flight

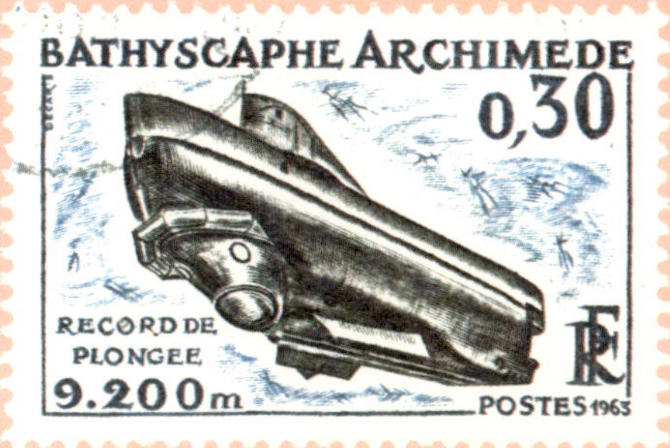

Archimède, holder of the deep sea diving record (9200 metres, 1963)

Conservation of forest trees

Past and present French colonies have given collectors many vivid pictures of local life and customs. *Left:* the eider duck is valued for its soft down. *Right:* extracting palm oil.

Somali Coast: wart hog

A Ferrari, one of a set issued for Monaco's 1967 Grand Prix

Italy

Vatican City · San Marino

It is still possible for every collector to start off the Italian pages of his album with stamps issued only one year after the very first Italian stamps of 1862. Used copies of the 1863 decorative numeral designs and portrait types of King Victor Emmanuel II are cheap. So are the many arms and portrait types which followed.

The most familiar modern Italian definitive is the portrait design taken from a coin of Syracuse, used on many face values for a number of years. Portraits of Julius Caesar, the Emperor Augustus, Romulus and Remus (believed to be the founders of Rome) and several sculptures of Michelangelo have also been used on definitive issues.

All the excitement of Italy's past is depicted, and the list of famous Italians whose portraits appear on the stamps reads like the all-star cast of some spectacular film. There is Mazzini, Cavour, Savonarola, astronomer Galileo, painters Michelangelo, Caravaggio, Raphael and Giotto, the poet Dante, explorer Marco Polo, and the national hero Giuseppe Garibaldi.

Collectors who buy mixed packets will be faced with a mass of tiny Italian stamps. To classify these correctly, keep an eye open for the words *segnatasse* (postage due) and *pacchi postale* (parcel post). *Posta pneumatica* indicates a stamp to cover the cost of delivery by the underground pneumatic tubes installed to carry letters from one post office to another in Italy's busiest cities.

VATICAN CITY

The Vatican City is a state within a state. It lies inside the city of Rome and issues its own stamps. As might be expected, the themes are religious, with portraits of saints, past Popes and churches.

SAN MARINO

This is another tiny scrap of a state lying on the Adriatic Coast of Italy. It has issued stamps since 1877.

ITALY	**First stamp issued: 1862** **Currency: 100 centesimi = 1 lira** **Inscription: Poste Italiane, Repubblica Italiana**
VATICAN CITY	**First stamp issued: 1929** **Currency: 100 centesimi = 1 lira** **Inscription: Poste Vaticane**
SAN MARINO	**First stamp issued: 1877** **Currency: 100 centesimi = 1 lira** **Inscription: San Marino**

5 common definitive types: an 1863 decorative numeral, 1901 arms type, Victor Emmanuel III, Syracuse coin design, and Julius Caesar (from the 'Imperial' series)

Sardinian shepherd

St Paul's route to Rome

Murray-Blenkinsop engine

Switzerland
Austria
Liechtenstein

SWITZERLAND

For the serious collector some of the most exciting 'classics' come from Switzerland. The Swiss cantons of Zurich, Basle and Geneva were ahead of most nations with the issue of the 'Zurich numerals' and 'double Genevas' in 1843, and the 'Basle doves' in 1845.

These are items that only collectors with well lined pocket-books can afford but there are many modern issues which make Switzerland a very good country for the small-budget collector.

Gay colours, good printing and interesting themes are what make modern Swiss stamps attractive

There are many charity issues. The 'Pro Juventute' stamps in aid of children's welfare are particularly popular. There are also fascinating publicity issues for events of national and international interest, like the opening of the Grand St Bernard road tunnel in 1964.

And there are, of course, stamps showing all the things for which Switzerland is famed: the spiky summit of the Matterhorn, typical Swiss chalets, cheese-making, an alpine hornblower, skaters and skiers, the edelweiss and the gentian.

Switzerland is also the headquarters of many international organisations which issue their own stamps.

AUSTRIA

Austria's most famous stamp is the rare six-kreuzer 'Mercury head' newspaper stamp of 1851. Today it is worth about £4,000.

Early definitives were mainly arms types and portraits of Emperor Franz Josef.

Two long definitive series worth trying to build into complete sets are the 1948 provincial costume series and the 1957 buildings series.

LIECHTENSTEIN

This is one of Europe's tiniest states, tucked between Austria and Switzerland. Like many pocket-handkerchief countries it produces stamps mainly for the revenue from sales to collectors.

SWITZERLAND	**First stamp issued: 1843 (canton)** **Currency: 100 centimes = 1 Swiss franc** **Inscription: Helvetia**
AUSTRIA	**First stamp issued: 1850** **Currency: 100 Groschen = 1 Schilling** **Inscription: Republik Österreich**
LIECHTENSTEIN	**First stamp issued: 1912** **Currency: 100 Rappen = 1 Swiss franc** **Inscription: Fürstentum Liechtenstein**

Buildings definitive: Neuchâtel

The Matterhorn

Charity issue: kingfisher

Costume design: Vienna

Heidenreichstein Castle

St Peter and St Paul

Germany

Germania

In 1872 several small states which had previously issued their own stamps united to form the German empire.

The new country's early designs included the well-known eagle emblem, numeral designs, and the 'Germania' head copied from a portrait of actress Anna Führing. They carry various inscriptions: *Deutschreichspost, Reichspost, Deutsches Reich.*

An interesting feature is the sudden rise in face values in the 1920s. At first it looks as if postage rates went mad. Low values were replaced by hundred-mark values, then by thousands, then by millions; and finally by milliards (a thousand million). The explanation is that the value of the German mark had fallen. Most of these seemingly high-value stamps are in fact very common and very cheap.

Once the currency was under control again low face values returned.

Portraits of President Hindenburg and Hitler dominate the definitive issues of the 1930s.

Classifying German stamps from 1945 onwards is one of the collector's puzzles. Their history was complicated because until 1949 several issuing zones existed.

From 1949 onwards the pattern is much simpler. In that year Germany divided into two parts, West Germany and East Germany. The stamps of West Germany, the Federal Republic, carry the words *Deutsche Bundespost*, and those of East Germany the words *Deutsche Demokratische Republik* or the letters D.D.R.

In addition, West Berlin has its own stamp issues which usually have the name Berlin somewhere in the inscription.

West Germany has many fine pictorial issues, generally agreed to be among the best designed and best printed in the world. They are so numerous that only an illustrated catalogue can suggest their enormous variety. Those illustrated on the opposite page give only the barest idea of the range of themes.

An unusually humorous stamp issued in 1970 shows Baron von Münchhausen, renowned for his exaggerated accounts of his exploits, riding unconcernedly on a horse that has been severed clean through the middle.

The stamps of East Germany are discussed on page 45.

First stamp issued: 1872
Currency: 100 Pfennigs = 1 Mark
Inscriptions: Deutschland, Reichspost, Deutschreichspost, Grossdeutschesreich, Deutsche Bundespost

The beginning of the rapid rise in face values

Inflation overprint

President Hindenburg

Adolf Hitler

Blacksmith and reaper designs 1921

West Berlin issues: the Philharmonia Hall and the motorway ('New Berlin' series), and the Brandenburg Gate

Left: Anglo-American military government issue 1945–6
Right: a French zone stamp for the Province of Baden

Left: 1945 issue for the Russian sector of Berlin
Right: 1949 bricklayer and reaper design for the American, British and Russian zones

Olympic Games 1960

An early Daimler

Charity stamp: Little Red Riding Hood

St George and the dragon

The Miracle of the Fishes

Bonn town hall

Portrait types: Queens Wilhelmina and Juliana

Netherlands Belgium Luxembourg

NETHERLANDS

Holland's first stamp was a portrait of King William II. Since then Dutch definitives have shown Queen Wilhelmina and the present queen, Queen Juliana, numeral and posthorn designs and – in recent years – small pictorial designs.

There are stamps which show the flowers and windmills for which Holland is traditionally famous, and others showing the polderland won back from the sea by dredging and building dykes.

Good pictorials to collect are the regional costume series (1960), beach and meadow birds (1961), Dutch aircraft (1968) and naval heroes (1943).

Charity stamps are issued every year in aid of children's welfare. Their subjects are light-hearted: gay goblins, fairy tale scenes and children playing. Some bear the words *Voor het Kind* ('for the children').

Stamps with the inscription *Cour Internationale de Justice* are the stamps of the International Court of Justice which meets in the Hague to discuss matters of international law.

Stamps inscribed *Nederland Indie, Nederland Nieuw Guinea* and *Nederlandse Antillen* are the stamps of Dutch colonies.

Numeral and small pictorial definitives

Charity stamp

BELGIUM

With Holland and Luxembourg, Belgium makes up the three Benelux countries (Be Belgium, Ne Nederland, and Lux Luxembourg).

Definitives show the king's head. Because Belgium's parcel post service is run by the state railways, there are special parcel stamps inscribed *post colli* and *colis postaux*.

William of Orange landing at Scheveningen

LUXEMBOURG

The Grand Duchy of Luxembourg is the third and smallest of the three Benelux countries. The official currency is the Belgian franc. Most of the definitives have shown the portrait of the ruling Grand Duke or Duchess.

Olympic Games diving event

Gerhardt Mercator

NETHERLANDS	**First stamp issued: 1852** **Currency: 100 cents=1 guilder** **Inscription: Nederland**
BELGIUM	**First stamp issued: 1849** **Currency: 100 centimes=1 Belgian franc** **Inscription: Belgie Belgique**
LUXEMBOURG	**First stamp issued: 1852** **Inscription: Luxembourg**

Denmark
Greenland
Iceland

The familiar caravel and Danish coat of arms

DENMARK

Denmark's stamps are well designed, neat and colourful, and with just over 500 stamps it makes a good choice for a special collection.

The first royal portraits appeared in 1904, and the first pictorial stamp in 1912.

A collection of all the variations of the early arms types, kings' heads and numerals would fill a whole album. Some are shown here. So is the famous caravel design first used in 1927. In a modified version the caravel is still going strong.

A strange but ingenious device for protecting the letters is shown on the 15 öre stamp (page 6) issued for the Danish Stamp Centenary in 1951. It is a mail cart carrying a large globular container. After complaints about letters reaching their destination sodden and battered in wet weather, they were given the protection of a sturdy globe suspended in the cart. The device was cumbersome but it worked.

King's head type: Christian X and Frederick IX

Niels Bohr, atomic scientist

GREENLAND

Greenland is a Danish possession importantly placed on trans-polar air routes. That five-sixths of its area is covered with a vast ice sheet could almost be guessed from its stamp designs of polar bears, eskimos, dog teams, seals, eider ducks, and whaling scenes. Even a recent definitive of King Frederick IX shows him wearing a hooded anorak.

The Wheel of Agriculture

ICELAND

There is plenty of drama in the stamps of this tiny republic: erupting volcanoes, hot springs, leaping salmon, powerful waterfalls, pony pack trains. The lot of the eighteenth-century Icelandic postman was pretty dramatic too, judging from the stamp shown here.

Before its independence in 1944 Iceland came under Danish rule, and definitives up to that time show the portrait of the kings of Denmark.

DENMARK	**First stamp issued: 1851** **Currency: 100 öre = 1 krone** **Inscription: Danmark**
GREENLAND	**First stamp issued: 1938** **Currency: 100 öre = 1 krone** **Inscription: Grønland**
ICELAND	**First stamp issued: 1873** **Currency: 100 aur = 1 krona** **Inscription: Island**

18th-century Icelandic postman

King Frederick IX

Sweden

Sweden's big stamp story, the story of the unique 3-skilling banco, has already been told on page 7. The design reappeared on two stamps issued in 1955 to celebrate the centenary of Swedish postage stamps.

The commonest definitive designs are the lion motif, the three crowns and the reigning monarch's head.

Now, like most other countries, Sweden introduces new designs fairly frequently. Recent definitives worth keeping a look-out for are the four fifth-century helmet designs (1967), the five wild flower designs (1968) and the five wildlife stamps issued in the same year.

One of the first features a new collector notices in Swedish stamps is the straight-cut or *imperforate* edges. Sweden does not print her stamps in sheets, but in coils or in booklet form. The coil stamps are imperforate on two parallel sides. Booklet stamps may be imperforate on one side or on 2 or 3 adjoining sides.

The Northern Countries Day stamps issued in 1964 and 1969 show the close links with Scandinavian neighbours Finland, Denmark, Norway and Iceland. All five used the same design printed with their own inscriptions.

Two 1958 stamps show the value of modern transport methods in winter. They commemorated the tenth anniversary of the first regular helicopter postal service linking many offshore islands with Stockholm. Until the service began, many of the inhabitants used to be cut off from the mainland in winter.

A design of special interest marking an unusual event is the publicity issue of 1967, when Sweden changed from driving on the left hand side of the road to the right. A special postmark was also used to remind drivers of the date of the change-over.

First stamp issued: 1855
Currency: 100 öre = 1 krona
Inscription: Sverige

3 definitive types: lion design, Swedish coat of arms, and a numeral motif

Stamp centenary issue

2 king's head types: Oscar II and Gustav VI

Helicopter postal service

Elk

Swedish flag issue

Publicity issue: to draw attention to a new road rule

Norway

Portrait types: Haakon VII and Olaf V

Even the least energetic collector can get together a reasonable collection of Norway's 700 stamps, starting from about 1900 and leaving the more expensive earlier issues aside.

Until 1905 Norway was united to the kingdom of Sweden. The stamps of this period show face values in skillings until 1877, and after that date in krona and ora.

As in the other Scandinavian countries there are many long definitive sets showing numeral designs, arms designs and the king's head. In one form or another the numeral type with a posthorn design has been used for a hundred years. Since 1962 small pictorial definitives have appeared.

Norway has its rare stamps, and it also has a very rare road, closely linked with stamps. For many years the North Cape, lying far within the Arctic Circle, was cut off each winter. In 1930 a special fund was started to raise enough money to build a road to the Cape. Special stamps carrying a surcharge were sold and in 1956 the road was completed.

Without doubt the most wholly 'polar' stamp is the airmail issue of 1925 showing a polar bear with raised head watching Roald Amundsen's plane passing overhead on its unsuccessful north polar flight in 1925. A year later, in 1926, with aviation pioneers Umberto Nobile and Lincoln Ellsworth, Amundsen made another – and this time successful – attempt to fly over the North Pole, from Spitsbergen to Alaska, in the Italian-built dirigible *Norge*. But even then, disappointment was Amundsen's. The American aviator Richard Byrd had already become the first man to fly over the Pole two days earlier.

Amundsen also figures on two stamps issued in 1961 to commemorate his arrival at the South Pole in 1911, after a grim race with Captain Scott to reach the Pole first.

An unusual commemorative shows Arne Garborg, the author who campaigned for his country's name to be spelled Noreg instead of Norge. The inscription used on the stamp is of course *Noreg*.

The inscription 'Offentlik Sak' (or O.S.) indicates an official stamp, while a white cross enclosed in a circle and surmounted by an eagle is the emblem of the Quisling government of World War II.

First stamp issued: 1855
Currency: 100 öre = 1 krone
Inscription: Norge, Noreg

Posthorn and coat of arms definitives

Small pictorial definitives: reef knot and rock drawings

Beehive, symbolising industry

Stave church

Roald Amundsen at the South Pole

Finland

Two arms type designs

The Mora stone

Red Cross stamp

Viking ships: Northern Countries Day issue, 1969

Pulp and paper reel

Tuberculosis Fund issue

Until 1917 Finland was a Grand Duchy of Russia, and early Finnish stamps show face values in roubles and kopeks, and depict the eagle of Imperial Russia.

The first stamp of independent Finland was the 1917 issue showing the familiar lion emblem, since used on a wide range of values and in a great many colours. Later definitive issues used the same emblem with slight changes in its design.

Modern Finnish stamps are neatly drawn and have delicate colours.

The Red Cross and Tuberculosis Relief Fund issues are well known. Stamps with appropriate designs and carrying a surcharge are issued regularly, and the money raised is paid to the funds. The Red Cross stamps always have the Red Cross symbol somewhere on them, and the Tuberculosis stamps have a small Cross of Lorraine.

Famous Finns appear, of course, on the nation's stamps. They include the composer Sibelius, author Zacharias Topelius, and actress Ida Aalberg. Although he was not Finnish, Martin Luther, the church reformer, is also honoured, on a stamp issued in 1967.

Many stamps show forestry and papermaking scenes, for Finland is the most densely wooded country in Europe and the forest is her most precious possession, providing wood for making paper, furniture and textiles.

More than one stamp has even been used as an admission ticket to an exhibition. One was the 1960 30-mark stamp issued on the occasion of the centenary of serpentine rouletting, a special 'wavy line' type of stamp separation for which early Finnish stamps were famous. For 150 marks visitors got one of the centenary stamps and admission to the exhibition.

Two others used as stamp exhibition tickets in the same way were the 1948 12-mark stamp showing a Finnish mail carrier's badge, and the 1956 issue commemorating the centenary of the first Finnish postage stamp.

Perhaps the most symbolic of all Finland's stamps is the 20-penni design issued to celebrate fifty years of independence. Its design represents 'Wood and Water' and is very fitting for a land of lakes and forests.

First stamp issued: 1856 (Grand Duchy), 1917 (Republic)
Currency: 100 kopeks = 1 rouble (Grand Duchy)
100 penni = 1 mark (Republic)
Inscription: Suomi-Finland

Eastern Europe

Albania · Bulgaria · Czechoslovakia East Germany · Greece · Hungary Poland · Rumania · Yugoslavia

When a stamp collector speaks of Eastern Europe he means all those countries which issue stamps under the direct or indirect influence of Russia. These are East Germany, Hungary, Bulgaria, Poland, Rumania, Yugoslavia, Albania and Czechoslovakia.

Greece lies geographically in eastern Europe but is not Russian controlled or influenced.

The *early* stamps of these countries before they came under Russian influence are of great interest to serious collectors just as other early stamps are. But the thousands of modern 'picture' stamps are another kettle of fish. Most of the eastern bloc countries issue attractive designs but they have a reputation for issuing far more than they need for true postal purposes. Large quantities of their stamps are sold direct to dealers and collectors cancelled with a clear and carefully placed cancellation mark without ever going through the mails.

Although the stamps have little collecting value in terms of money, they give the topic or thematic collector a lot of useful picture themes, and provided he knows that they are not likely to increase much in value, then they are well worth collecting just for the fun of the subjects.

Only Czechoslovakia has kept its tradition for good designs and well printed stamps. The subjects are well chosen and they give the rest of the world a chance to see the work of artists who would otherwise be almost unknown outside their own country.

Identifying eastern European stamps is the first thing to learn, and is an easy matter once you know the key word to look for in each case.

East German stamps are marked DDR, standing for Deutsche Demokratische Republik (German Democratic Republic). Those of Hungary usually have the word 'Magyar' somewhere on them. Poland is Polska. Rumania is Romania, Romana, Romina or Romine, Czechoslovakia is Ceskoslovensko, Yugoslavia is Jugoslavija, or Hrvatska on early stamps. Greece is Hellas. Albania's inscriptions include the word Shqiperia, Shqiperise, or Shqipni.

Currency:

Albania: 100 qint=1 lek
Bulgaria: 100 stotinki=1 lev
Czechoslovakia: 100 heller=1 crown
East Germany: 100 (DN) pfennig=1 (DN) mark
Greece: 100 lepta=1 drachma
Hungary: 100 filler=1 forint
Poland: 100 groszy=1 zloty
Rumania: 100 bani=1 leu
Yugoslavia: 100 paras=1 dinar

Sunflower harvester

City of Olomuc

Peregrine falcon

Racing cyclist. International Peace Cycle Race, 1962

'History of tennis' series

25-qint opah fish. 1967 series

Radio tower, 1967

Russia

Russia is a vast country and has issued an enormous number of stamps – over 4,000 so far – and is adding more each year.

The spread eagle emblem of Imperial Russia was the first design used. This was followed by portraits of the last of the Czars, Nicholas II. As the fortunes of the Empire declined some stamps were overprinted on the back to serve as paper money.

In 1917 a revolt by the Bolsheviks overthrew the Czars, and Russia became a republic. The new state's first stamp showed a symbolic sword hacking free the chains of slavery.

In 1923 the Union of Soviet Socialist Republics (U.S.S.R.) was created. New issues became more frequent and the stamps quickly began to show the pictorial and political pattern that is now familiar.

Russia is a classic example of a country that uses stamps for political propaganda. Her stamp history bristles with scenes of military exploits, war heroes and long series of war medals. Almost all the stamps proclaim the glory of some purely Russian success. But in spite of the propaganda, they give a glimpse of life in a country that is still little known, and in this respect they are fascinating.

There are one or two non-Russian celebrities who have been given 'stamp space'. They include Charles Darwin, the scientist who first put forward the idea that man had descended from the apes, the Norwegian explorer Fridjhof Nansen, the famous Italian actress Eleanora Duse, and her compatriot Garibaldi. The composer Chopin, the novelist Charles Dickens and the poet John Milton are also commemorated.

Very few people outside Russia speak the Russian language and therefore few can understand the inscriptions on the stamps. To try to overcome this problem there have been Russian stamps with inscriptions printed in Esperanto in the hope that they would be understood by more collectors.

First stamp issued: 1858
Currency: 100 kopeks = 1 rouble
Inscription: CCCP

Czar Nicholas and the Imperial arms, two stamps of Imperial Russia

4-kopek snow tractor design. Arctic and Antarctic research series, 1963

May Day procession in Moscow

Mi-10 helicopter. 12 kopek air stamp

Athletes. 4-kopek triangular, 1966

The Middle East

Iran · Iraq · Israel · Jordan · Lebanon · Saudi Arabia · Syria · Turkey

The 'Middle East' is a useful omnibus term that covers Iran, Iraq, Israel, the Lebanon, Saudi Arabia, Syria and Turkey, as well as a multitude of tiny oil sheikdoms with a growing habit of issuing stamps almost as big as themselves.

Most countries in this part of the world are Arab states, and therefore most of the older stamps have inscriptions in Arabic only. Care and an illustrated catalogue will help to identify them correctly.

Signs of France's former influence in the Middle East can be seen in the stamps of Syria and Lebanon. Both came under French control after World War 1 and their early issues were French types overprinted for local use. The sower and Pasteur types shown on page 34 were two designs used.

Lebanese stamps still show their French ancestry in their inscription, which gives the name of the country in French (*Liban*) as well as in Arabic.

Syria shook off her French inscription after uniting with Egypt to form the United Arab Republic in 1958 to 1961. Stamps of this period are inscribed UAR. In 1961 the inscription Syrian Arab Republic was adopted and is still used.

For the collector by far the most interesting Middle East country is Israel, the Jewish state that was created in 1948. Since its first issue it has set a high standard of design that has given pleasure to collectors all over the world.

The celebration of the New Year each autumn is an important event in the Jewish calendar and just as many Christian countries have special Christmas stamps, so Israel issues New Year stamps. Subjects have included ancient Hebrew seals, the scrolls of the Torah, and a set of six illustrating the Creation (Light, Heaven, Earth, Stars, Man, and Birds and Beasts).

A Saudi Arabian stamp of equal religious interest depicts the Ka'aba or Black Stone of Mecca, the holy city of the Mohammedans. The Black Stone is believed to have been given to Abraham by Gabriel and each year is covered with a new black brocade cover called the *kiswa*. Mecca is Mohammed's birthplace and the direction in which all Mohammedans turn to pray.

Currency:
Iran: 100 dinars = 1 rial
Iraq: 1000 fils = 1 dinar
Israel: 100 agorot = 1 Israeli pound
Jordan: 1000 fils = 1 dinar
Lebanon: 100 centimes = 1 piastre
Saudi Arabia: 800 piastres = 1 gold sovereign
Syria: 100 centimes = 1 piastre
Turkey: 100 kurus = 1 lira

Jordan: King Hussein

Iran: The Shah of Persia

Israel: young immigrant

Syria: an ancient vessel

Turkey: Kemal Ataturk statue

Lebanon: butterfly airstamp series, 1965

Iraq: census graph, 1965

Southern Africa

The Republic of South Africa
South West Africa · Botswana
Lesotho · Swaziland

Springbok: bilingual pair

Triangular 'Hope' design

Dromedaris

Natal kingfisher

Voortrekker wagon crossing the Drakensberg

Letter carrier

Botswana provisional

THE REPUBLIC OF SOUTH AFRICA

It was a Dutch doctor, Jan van Riebeeck, who set up the first European settlement on the tip of Africa. In 1672 the Dutch East India Company sent him to establish a place where its ships could take on board fresh water and provisions on their way to the spice islands of the Far East.

One of van Riebeeck's ships was the *Goede Hoop*, named after the Cape of Good Hope.

When British settlers arrived there was friction with the Boers, who finally made their Great Trek over the Drakensberg Mountains to settle in Orange Free State, the Transvaal and Natal.

Each of the early colonies had its own stamps, the most famous of which were the Cape triangulars, first issued in 1853 to help native postal sorters who could not read to distinguish between local letters and others.

The British and Dutch colonies united in 1910 to form the Union of South Africa, and stamps were inscribed in both Afrikaans and English – or in Afrikaans and English on alternate stamps on a sheet.

Common early definitives include the springbok (the national emblem), an orange tree, and van Riebeeck's ship *Dromedaris*. A later series shows South Africa's famous wild life.

There are also stamps showing gold and diamond mining.

The Boers' Trek is commemorated on many issues with wagons, trek carts, the Voortrekker Monument in Pretoria, and settlers' homesteads.

A stamp depicting a human heart commemorates the early heart transplant operations performed by South African surgeon Christian Barnard.

SOUTH WEST AFRICA

This was once a German colony using overprinted German and South African stamps. Now it has its own.

LESOTHO, BOTSWANA, SWAZILAND

Two British Commonwealth countries changed their names when they became independent. Basutoland became Lesotho, and Bechuanaland became Botswana. Swaziland, although now independent, kept its old name. All three use the same currency: the South African rand.

REPUBLIC OF SOUTH AFRICA

First stamp issued: 1870
Currency: 100 cents = 1 rand
Inscription: RSA, South Africa, Suid Afrika, Zuid Afrika

Eastern Africa

Ethiopia · Kenya · Malawi
Rhodesia · Somali
Tanzania · Uganda · Zambia

ETHIOPIA, AFARS AND ISSAS, SOMALIA
Ethiopia is one of the few countries still ruled by an emperor, Emperor Haile Selassie, whose portrait appears on many issues.

The Afars and Issas is the new name for what was once French Somaliland. The Somali Republic is the merger of former British Somaliland and Italian Somalia.

KENYA, UGANDA, TANZANIA
Designs include Mount Kenya, snow-capped Kilimanjaro, the craggy Mountains of the Moon, giant cacti, elephants, giraffes, lions and other big game.

Although these three countries now share the same postal system and the stamps carry all three countries' names, Kenya and Uganda had separate issues in the past. Tanzania is a 'young' state, created in 1965 from what had been Tanganyika and Zanzibar, the 'isle of cloves'.

MOZAMBIQUE AND MALAGASY REPUBLIC
Mozambique is a large Portuguese overseas province with many colourful stamp issues.

The Malagasy Republic is made up of Madagascar and one or two smaller islands in the Indian Ocean.

RHODESIA, MALAWI AND ZAMBIA
Rhodesia's first stamps were inscribed 'British South Africa Company', the trading company which administered the territory. Later there were separate issues for North and South Rhodesia. Then came joint issues with neighbouring Nyasaland. Finally, from 1964 onwards, there were separate issues again, when Southern Rhodesia became plain Rhodesia, Nyasaland became Malawi, and Northern Rhodesia became Zambia.

Malawi already has a long backlist of pictorial stamps. One of the most interesting issues is the first decimal series in 1971, showing 13 different gazelles.

The names of the new coins are interesting too. The word *tambala* means cockerel, and *kwacha* means dawn, the hour at which the cock crows.

Zambia's first stamp showed the dramatic Victoria Falls and the President. Values were first shown in shillings and pence but are now in decimal currency.

Currency:

Ethiopia: 100 cents = 1 Ethiopian dollar
Afars: 100 centimes = 1 franc
Somali: 100 centesimi = 1 Somali shilling
Kenya, Uganda, Tanzania: 100 cents = 1 shilling
Mozambique: 100 centavos = 1 escudo
Malawi: 100 tambalas = 1 kwacha
Zambia: 100 ngwee = 1 kwacha

Tobacco fields

Uganda: sacred ibis

Kenya: Thomson's gazelle

3-state issue: mountaineering

Malawi: timber industry

Emperor Haile Selassie

Zambia: Angoni warrior

North Africa

Algeria · Egypt · Libya · Morocco Sudan · Tunisia

The arms of Libya

Moorish arch

Moulay Ismail

The city of Kairouan

Egyptian pharaoh

Sudanese cotton picker

CENTRAL AFRICA

Traditional musical instrument series

Refrigeration in Chad's meat industry

ALGERIA

Centuries ago the Algerian ports were pirate strongholds. Later, French colonists created prosperous fruit farms and vineyards along the coast.

Look for stamps showing the soldiers of the famous French Foreign Legion that had its H.Q. in Algiers. And for the cameleers, the Tuareg tribesmen, the fennec or desert fox, the ostrich and the mouflon (a big-horned wild sheep).

EGYPT

Once a kingdom and now the United Arab Republic, Egypt has issued many stamps since its first pictorial 'sphinx and pyramid' issue in 1867. By far the most interesting are those showing the pharaohs and the ancient Egyptian gods. There is Osiris, god of the Nile, and Isis his wife, Thoth the dog-headed ape god, Anubis the jackal-headed god, and Re the sun god.

Modern Egypt is represented by cotton fields, the Suez Canal, the Nile Hilton Hotel, and the giant Aswan Dam.

UAR is the inscription that identifies recent issues.

LIBYA

This is a former Italian colony. Below the dry Libyan desert lies the main source of the country's wealth: oil. And oil is a theme that recurs on the stamps, in the form of giant oil rigs, huge tankers and endless pipelines.

MOROCCO

Once part of Morocco was a French colony and part of it was Spanish. Now it is a kingdom ruled by Hassan II. Look for the inscription *Royaume du Maroc* to identify recent issues.

SUDAN

Although the camel postman is by far the best known Sudanese design, the present republic issues many pictorials of interest to the topic collector.

TUNISIA

Like Algeria, Tunisia was once a French colony but is now independent.

Currency:

Algeria: 100 centimes = 1 dinar
Eygpt: 100 piastres=£1 Egyptian
Libya: 1000 milliemes=£1 Libyan
Morocco: 100 Moroccan francs=1 dirham
Sudan: 10 milliemes=1 piastre
Tunisia: 1000 millimes=1 dinar

West and central Africa

Angola · Central African Republic · Chad · Congo · Gambia Ghana · Guinea · Liberia · Mali · Niger · Nigeria · Senegal Sierra Leone · Togo · Volta

WEST AFRICA

There are now just under 20 states in West Africa producing stamps, from Spanish Sahara in the north to Angola in the south. Less than 20 years ago only Liberia, a small state created for freed Negro slaves, was an independent country. Now almost all the former European colonies are independent.

New states are usually enthusiastic producers of large, bright pictorials, and the new states of Africa are no exception. They have between them produced a flood of new designs, many of them showing the part modern science and modern equipment play in farming, industry and the daily life of the people.

Senegal, Mali, Guinea, Ivory Coast, Togo, Dahomey, Cameroons, Mauritania, Volta, Gaboon and Niger were French possessions, and these are still the countries which offer the most interesting issues for the collector who specialises in 'life in other lands'.

Ghana (formerly the Gold Coast), Nigeria, the Gambia and Sierra Leone (the first country in the world to issue 'free shape' stamps) were once British colonies.

Portugal's colonies were Portuguese Guinea and Angola (now overseas provinces) while Spain held Spanish Sahara, Ifni, Rio Muni and Fernando Poo. The last two united and now issue stamps as Equatorial Guinea.

CENTRAL AFRICA

In the heart of Africa but with a narrow outlet to the Atlantic Ocean is what was once the Belgian Congo, now divided into Congo (capital Kinshasa) and the Republic of the Congo (capital Brazzaville).

The Central African Republic and Chad complete the list of French territories now enjoying republic status, while east of the Central African Republic lie Rwanda and Burundi, two tiny states formed from what was once a single country, Ruanda-Urundi.

Currency:

Cameroons, Central African Republic, Chad, Congo, Dahomey, Guinea, Ivory Coast, Mali, Mauritania, Niger, Senegal, Togo, Volta: 100 centimes = 1 franc

Angola: 100 centavos = 1 escudo
Equatorial Guinea: 100 centimos = 1 peseta
Gambia: 100 bututs = 1 dalasi
Liberia: 100 cents = 1 Liberian dollar
Nigeria: 12 pence = 1 Nigerian shilling
Sierra Leone: 100 cents = 1 leone

Liberia: African elephant

Congo Republic: cutting sugar cane

Mali: anti-locust campaign

Ghana: cocoa is a major crop

Gaboon: tropical fruit series (postage due stamps)

Nigeria: potter at work

The United States

George Washington, Abraham Lincoln and Thomas Jefferson, designs from 3 definitive series

Credo series (1960): George Washington

Credo series: Abraham Lincoln

Credo series: Thomas Jefferson

Portraits of George Washington and Benjamin Franklin were the designs of the first American national stamps in 1847, although for two years before that some postmasters, including the postmaster of New York, had been issuing their own local stamps.

At first postal charges covered only the cost of delivery from one post office to another. Private carrier companies took the letters on the last stage of their journey, adding their own special stamps to cover the cost. These carrier stamps are now rare and valuable.

Rebel stamps issued by the Confederates during the American Civil War are also rare and valuable.

The first attempt at an airmail flight was made by a balloonist, John Wise, who in 1859 set off from Lafayette, Indiana, in the balloon *Jupiter* carrying letters. Instead of going east, as he had calculated, the balloon headed south. Finally he had to throw the mails over the side. The one letter known to have survived is now worth thousands of pounds.

The attractive thing about American stamps is that although there are, of course, many expensive items, most of the stamps are cheap, easy to find and full of interest.

Whoever collects American commemoratives fills an album with American history from the landing of the Pilgrim Fathers up to the landing of the first man on the moon. Few countries have given such a clear and cxciting account of their past on stamps.

There's Columbus, the pioneers of the Far West, covered wagons, an Indian chief, a Pony Express rider, General Jackson leading his men into battle, log cabins, skyscrapers, Mississippi steamboats, baseball players and spaceflights.

It is very easy to get carried away by the commemoratives and forget the definitives. But there are several long series which deserve to be built into complete sets. Their subjects are past presidents, prominent Americans and national monuments. It is best to pick one of the series and concentrate on making it as complete as possible. With the help of an illustrated stamp catalogue the style of each series soon becomes familiar. Examples from three of them are shown in the portraits on this page.

First stamp issued: 1847
Currency: 100 cents=1 U.S. dollar
Inscription: U.S. Postage

John Kennedy memorial issue

Settlers' wagon and Mount Hood

State charter of Carolina

Special delivery stamp

Christmas issue: the angel Gabriel

Tlingit totem, Alaska

Battle of Gettysburg commemorative

Panama Canal Zone stamp

1969 moon landing, printed from a die actually taken on the flight

Flag issue, July 4 1960

The first mail-carrying balloon flight

Publicity issue

South America

Argentina · Bolivia · Brazil · Chile Colombia · Ecuador · Guyana Paraguay · Peru · Surinam Uruguay · Venezuela

Argentina: prize bull

Argentina: San Martin

Brazil was the world's second nation to issue adhesive stamps – its famous 'bull's eyes' of 1843, and Bolivar, a department of Colombia, produced the world's smallest stamp with its first issue in 1863, a stamp of less than one third of an inch square.

Uruguay issued some unusual stamps in 1929, the triangular 'farmers' parcel stamps' for use on packages of farm produce. Their purpose was to encourage farmers to despatch their products to the towns.

By far the most frequent theme on South American stamps is liberty. There are hundreds of stamps with portraits of national heroes who fought for independence, first against Spain and Portugal, and later against harsh and unjust governments. The three heroes most often depicted are General Bolivar of Venezuela, General San Martin of Argentina, and Bernardo O'Higgins in Chile.

Maps, flags, coats of arms, religious subjects and air flight are the other themes that recur. It is easy to understand how important the aeroplane has been to South America, where land travel is made difficult by high mountains, dense forests and bleak grasslands – to say nothing of hostile Indian tribes.

The main sources of each country's wealth are also depicted: tin mining in Bolivia, beef cattle in Argentina, coffee in Brazil, oil in Venezuela, and copper in Chile.

Recent designs include many sports stamps and highly colourful series of tropical birds and animals.

Guyana (British Guiana until 1966) has the distinction of being the source of the world's rarest stamp, the 1-cent British Guiana issue of 1856, which it reproduced on two commemoratives in 1967. A detail from one of these appears on page 7.

Surinam (formerly Dutch Guiana) follows the style of Dutch designs, while French Guiana still uses French stamps.

Bolivia: revolutionaries

Brazil: Rio de Janeiro

Brazil: Ruy Barbosa

Brazil: patriot Henrique Dias

Currency:

Argentina: 100 centavos = 1 peso
Bolivia: 100 centavos = 1 peso
Brazil: 100 centavos = 1 cruzeiro
Chile: 100 centesimos = 1 escudo
Colombia: 100 centavos = 1 peso
Ecuador: 100 centavos = 1 sucre
Guyana: 100 cents = 1 Guyanan dollar
Paraguay: 100 centimos = 1 guarani
Peru: 100 centavos = 1 peso
Surinam: 100 cents = 1 gulden
Uruguay: 100 centesimos = 1 peso
Venezuela: 100 centimos = 1 bolivar

Chile: O'Higgins

Chile: locomotive

Colombia: Christmas stamp

Ecuador: UNESCO headquarters, Paris

Guyana: 1968 animal series

Surinam: bauxite mining

Paraguay: Human Rights Year.
United Nations emblem and flag

Peru: Simon Bolivar

Peru: Columbus's three ships

Uruguay: an early definitive

Uruguay: General Artigas dictating orders

Venezuela: air stamp

Central America

Costa Rica · Cuba
Guatemala · Honduras · Mexico
Nicaragua · Panama · Salvador

Panama: Chorerra Falls

Mexico: The volcano Popocatepetl Airstamp 1934

Guatemala: giant Mayan stone monument

El Salvador: Atlacatl

Dutch Antilles: typical Dutch house fronts

Nicaragua: Central American Common Market countries

Eight countries make up Central America. With the exception of Mexico they are mainly small republics, all vigorous stamp producers issuing gay pictorials far oftener than is needed for their postal purposes.

British Honduras, the only Commonwealth country in Central America, has stamps depicting her main products: mahogany, palm nuts, chicle (used in chewing gum) and grapefruit. A fine set of tropical birds in 1962 and a set of animals in 1968 give a colourful view of local wildlife.

Honduras is a small republic whose stamps should not be confused with the similarly named *British* Honduras.

Salvador, the smallest state in Central America, is almost as famous for revolutions as for coffee. Many of her stamps are now designed to attract tourists with animal and flower designs.

Nicaragua, the least populated of the republics, depicts her important products: bananas, sugar cane, coffee and cotton.

Guatemalan designs often incorporate the quetzal bird, the national emblem. *Quetzal* is also the name given to Guatemala's main unit of currency.

Costa Rica, which means 'rich coast', is also an agricultural land and stamp designs include coffee plantations, pineapples, tobacco and bananas.

Mexico is the richest of the Central American states. Early issues show the national hero Hidalgo and numeral designs. Modern issues are strong on sporting events, like the Olympic Games, held in Mexico in 1968, and the World Cup Football competition, held there in 1970.

A narrow strip of land on each side of the Panama Canal is controlled by the United States, which issues stamps inscribed 'Canal Zone'. These should be mounted with other United States issues.

Cuba, Haiti and the Dominican Republic are three busy Caribbean stamp producers. Their large pictorials are of interest mainly to topic collectors. Many of the Cuban issues have a strong political theme.

Puerto Rico, another Caribbean island, uses stamps issued by the United States.

Currency: **British Honduras: 100 cents = 1 dollar**
Costa Rica: 100 centimos = 1 colon
Cuba: 100 centavos = 1 peso
Dominican Republic: 100 centavos = 1 peso
Guatemala: 100 centavos = 1 quetzal
Haiti: 100 centimes = 1 gourde
Honduras: 100 centavos = 1 lempira
Mexico: 100 centavos = 1 peso
Nicaragua: 100 centavos = 1 cordoba
Panama: 100 centesimos = 1 balboa
Salvador: 100 centavos = 1 colon

China

Hong Kong · Korea · Macao
Mongolia

China is a vast country with a population of more than seven hundred million people. Once it was a single country ruled by the Emperor. Today there are two Chinas: the People's Republic of China, and the Nationalist Republic of China (or Taiwan).

Stamps of Imperial China included portraits of Confucius the sage, junks, ricefields, and the Temple of Heaven. The first airmail issue showed a mixture of old and new – a plane over the Great Wall of China, built thousands of years ago to keep out the Mongols.

THE CHINESE PEOPLE'S REPUBLIC

The designs are similar to those of other communist countries. There are portraits of Karl Marx, Stalin and Mao-tse Tung, and dozens of large pictorials of eager farm and factory workers, armies on the march, and successes in sport and science. There are also many issues of interest to the topic collector, including landscapes, the giant panda, Chinese flowers and goldfish, and some charming pictures of children.

THE NATIONALIST REPUBLIC (TAIWAN)

The portrait of General Chiang Kai Shek, the president, appears on many of the definitives. One of the most interesting designs is copied from an ancient hand scroll and shows a panoramic view spread over 5 or 6 stamps.

HONG KONG, MACAO, MONGOLIA

The name Hong Kong means 'Fragrant Harbour'. Because it is a British colony, it has used the portrait of the ruling British monarch through five reigns. There are also attractive pictorials.

Macao is a tiny Portuguese territory on the Chinese mainland.

Mongolia is an independent republic lying between China and Russia. Present-day designs show Russian influence but there are many large pictorials for the topic collector.

KOREA

There are now two Koreas, North and South. The stamps of North Korea have obvious military themes. Those of South Korea have a more general interest.

Currency: Chinese People's Republic: 100 fen=1 yuan
Nationalist Republic of China: 100 cents=1 silver yuan
Hong Kong: 100 cents=1 HK dollar
Macao: 100 avos=1 pataca
Mongolia: 100 mung=1 tahrik
North Korea: 100 chon=1 won
South Korea: 10 hwan=1 won

Chinese Imperial Post: 1898 dragon design

China: Dr Sun Yat Sen

China: The Great Wall of China, overprinted 'air post paid to Japan'.

Province of Manchuria: dragon dance

China: General Mao-tse Tung

South Korea: new currency definitive, 1962

Mongolia: Olympic Games 1960

Japan

Left: Japanese Imperial Post: chrysanthemum
Right: Tosho temple gateway

Himeji Castle

A temple figure

Chrysanthemum definitive

Mount Fuji, one of the numerous National Parks designs

Savings publicity stamp

The first Japanese stamps are known as 'Dragons' because these fabulous beasts formed part of the border design. They were followed by the famous 'Cherry Blossom' stamps in 1872, which featured Japan's national emblem, the chrysanthemum, for the first time. This motif was used regularly from then on until about 1948.

It is difficult to say which is the most familiar subject of Japanese stamps, the chrysanthemum or the snow-capped volcano Mount Fuji which overlooks Tokyo. Both have figured on so many issues.

Some of the world's first bird stamps came from Japan. The wild goose, the wagtail, cranes and the mandarin duck were favourite subjects for the early issues.

The main religions of Japan are Shintoism and Buddhism. Buddha appears on numerous stamps in various forms, and there are countless shrines, temples, pagodas and ornamental gates.

The Japanese are an artistic people and this can be seen in the delicate engraving of the early stamps as well as in the design and colours of modern issues.

Famous Japanese paintings and art treasures are well represented, and so are the National Parks which have been the theme of a long series begun in 1936, showing splendid lakes, majestic forests and impressive mountains and volcanoes.

There is a regular New Year greetings issue, usually depicting gay toys, for the New Year is the time for present-giving in Japan.

There are also stamps commemorating the National Athletics Championships each year.

Although there are so many stamps recalling Japan's oriental past, it is also a very 'modern' country. Everywhere a 'westernised' way of life exists side by side with the old traditional ways. Japan's express trains are among the fastest in the world, and many of her busy industries have the most modern equipment. So, alongside the temple statues and Mount Fuji stamp designs, there are express motorways, nuclear ships, modern bridges and tunnels, and space satellites.

First stamp issued: 1871
Currency: 100 sen = 1 yen
Inscription: Nippon

India Pakistan

Afghanistan · Bhutan · Burma Ceylon · Nepal

While India was part of the British Empire the stamps usually portrayed the British monarch in full regalia. Pictorial issues were rare. More varied designs were issued after the country was split into the two states of India and Pakistan.

Both countries issue fairly 'serious' stamps depicting their efforts to become modern states. There are stamps showing efforts to teach people how to read, and to stamp out the diseases (especially malaria) which have plagued both countries for centuries. There are others showing new tractors and modern factories.

The most attractive Indian pictorials date from the beginning of the Republic in 1950. One of the most exciting shows the conquest of Everest in 1953.

AFGHANISTAN

The 'tigers' are Afghanistan's best-known stamps, so named after the tiger's head design. Few whole 'tigers' are to be found because the local method of cancelling them was to tear a small portion out of the stamp itself.

BURMA

Once Burma produced good definitives but since independence has issued few stamps.

CEYLON

Ceylon's contribution to the collector's stamp picture of the East includes the famous Temple of the Tooth Kandyan dancers, tea plantations, rice harvesting and elephants.

NEPAL AND BHUTAN

These two tiny states lie locked in the Himalayas. It is therefore surprising to find that Bhutan has some very 'with it' stamps printed on plastic to give a 3D effect. The reason is that Bhutan's stamp production is handled by an agency outside Bhutan.

Recent issues of Nepal feature King Mahendra and Queen Ratna.

PAKISTAN

Although part of India divides East Pakistan from West Pakistan, they both use the same stamps.

Currency: **Afghanistan: 100 pouls=1 afghani**
Bhutan: 100 chetrum=1 rupee
Burma: 100 pyas=1 kyat
Ceylon: 100 cents=1 rupee
India: 100 paise = 1 rupee
Nepal: 100 pice=1 rupee
Pakistan: 100 paise=1 rupee

Stamp centenary. Postal transport in 1854

Sher Shar Suri

Independence anniversary: national industries

Afghanistan's national game, buskaski

Orchid definitive

Rice planting in Burma

South-east Asia

Cambodia · Indonesia · Laos
Malaysia · Thailand · Vietnam

Indonesia. *Left:* President Sokaerno
Right: 11th Colombo Plan issue

Penang and Malacca state issues of the same design

Singapore: sports festival 1970

National Rubber Conference, 1968: tapping rubber and aircraft tyres

Malaysia: Johor issue of a design used by other members of the Malaysian Federation

South-east Asia is an area of twisted land shapes and odd groups of islands best described as 'south of China' and 'east of India'.

LAOS
This former French colony is now an independent kingdom. Buddhism, the main religion, is depicted on many stamps in the form of statues of Buddha, legends and temples.

Laotian stamps are large and gay. Subjects include rice cultivation, native musicians, and musical instruments, animals and birds, fruits and flowers.

VIETNAM
There are two Vietnams, North and South. The stamps of North Vietnam are mostly war propaganda issues with anti-American themes. They are identified by the inscription *Viet nam Dan Chu Cong hoa* (Democratic Republic of Vietnam). The designs of South Vietnam carry the inscription *Viet nam Cong Hoa* (Republic of Vietnam).

CAMBODIA
Another old French colony that won its independence. The first stamps were issued in 1951.

THAILAND
The early stamps of Thailand (once Siam) showed her king. Modern pictorials depict Thai buildings, traditional festivals and exotic dances. A series in 1968 showed Queen Sirikit wearing different Thai costumes.

MALAYSIA AND SINGAPORE
Malaysia includes the nine Federated States of Malaya, as well as Singapore, Sabah and Sarawak. Because the many small states have at some time or other all produced their own stamps this is a difficult area for the collector to sort out without the help of an illustrated catalogue.

INDONESIA
This is another republic made up of several smaller territories: Java, Sumatra, the Celebes and Moluccas islands, and part of Borneo.

Currency: Cambodia: 100 cents=1 riel
Indonesia: 100 sen=1 rupiah
Laos: 100 cents=1 kip
Malaysia: 100 cents=1 Malaysian dollar
Singapore: 100 cents=1 Singapore dollar
Thailand: 100 satangs=1 baht
Vietnam (North): 100 xu=1 dong
Vietnam (South): 100 cents=1 piastre

Brunei: the sultan

Sabah: overprint on North Borneo issue

Philippines: volcanic eruption, 1965

Democratic Republic of Vietnam: traditional sword fighting

Vietnam: javelin thrower

New Hebrides: spear fisherman

Thailand:
King Bhumibol

Cambodia: Buddhist temple

Papua and New Guinea: publicity issue for higher education

Nauru: black lizard

Olympic Games souvenir cover.
France, 1968

A miniature sheet from Samoa and Sisifo for Interpex 1971

A Dutch first day cover franked with five stamps designed by computer. 1970